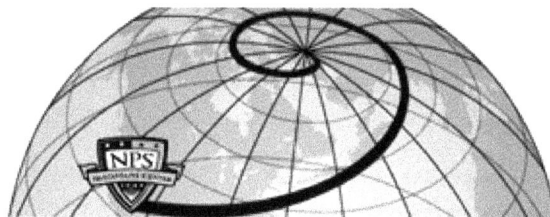

NAVAL
POSTGRADUATE
SCHOOL

MONTEREY, CALIFORNIA

THESIS

**SMALL COMBATANTS FOR THE HOMELAND
DEFENSE MISSION**

by

Andrew M. Brown

March 2013

Thesis Advisor: James C. Moltz
Second Reader: Wayne Hughes

THIS PAGE INTENTIONALLY LEFT BLANK

REPORT DOCUMENTATION PAGE		*Form Approved OMB No. 0704-0188*

Public reporting burden for this collection of information is estimated to average 1 hour per response, including the time for reviewing instruction, searching existing data sources, gathering and maintaining the data needed, and completing and reviewing the collection of information. Send comments regarding this burden estimate or any other aspect of this collection of information, including suggestions for reducing this burden, to Washington headquarters Services, Directorate for Information Operations and Reports, 1215 Jefferson Davis Highway, Suite 1204, Arlington, VA 22202-4302, and to the Office of Management and Budget, Paperwork Reduction Project (0704-0188) Washington DC 20503.

1. AGENCY USE ONLY *(Leave blank)*	2. REPORT DATE March 2013	3. REPORT TYPE AND DATES COVERED Master's Thesis
4. TITLE AND SUBTITLE SMALL COMBATANTS FOR THE HOMELAND DEFENSE MISSION		**5. FUNDING NUMBERS**
6. AUTHOR(S) Andrew M. Brown		
7. PERFORMING ORGANIZATION NAME(S) AND ADDRESS(ES) Naval Postgraduate School Monterey, CA 93943-5000		**8. PERFORMING ORGANIZATION REPORT NUMBER**
9. SPONSORING /MONITORING AGENCY NAME(S) AND ADDRESS(ES) N/A		**10. SPONSORING/MONITORING AGENCY REPORT NUMBER**

11. SUPPLEMENTARY NOTES The views expressed in this thesis are those of the author and do not reflect the official policy or position of the Department of Defense or the U.S. Government. IRB Protocol number ____N/A____.

12a. DISTRIBUTION / AVAILABILITY STATEMENT Approved for public release; distribution is unlimited	12b. DISTRIBUTION CODE

13. ABSTRACT (maximum 200 words)
This thesis examines how the composition of the U.S. fleet, with specific focus on small combatants, affects the ability of the United States Navy to undertake homeland defense missions and provides suggestions to improve its core competency.

Currently, the U.S. Navy relies on a shrinking group of aging Oliver Hazard Perry class frigates to conduct counter-piracy, counter-narcotics, counter maritime insurgency, and maritime engagement missions. The large warships that make up the rest of the fleet are able to undertake these missions, but their cost and capabilities make them better suited for other operations. This thesis examines the proposed Littoral Combat Ship but argues that it is not the ideal ship: it is too expensive, too vulnerable, and undermanned, and it has a modular concept that is too underdeveloped for practical naval operations. Instead, this thesis proposes that the U.S. Navy would be better served by procuring a traditional frigate or corvette to accomplish the variety of missions that fall under the umbrella of homeland defense. Such a traditional small combatant would provide the U.S. Navy with a warship capable of conducting traditional fleet operations as well as operating at the lower end of the spectrum of operations.

14. SUBJECT TERMS Navy, Maritime Security, Frigate, Littoral Combat Ship, Homeland Defense	15. NUMBER OF PAGES 101
	16. PRICE CODE

17. SECURITY CLASSIFICATION OF REPORT Unclassified	18. SECURITY CLASSIFICATION OF THIS PAGE Unclassified	19. SECURITY CLASSIFICATION OF ABSTRACT Unclassified	20. LIMITATION OF ABSTRACT UU

NSN 7540-01-280-5500

Standard Form 298 (Rev. 2-89)
Prescribed by ANSI Std. 239-18

THIS PAGE INTENTIONALLY LEFT BLANK

SMALL COMBATANTS FOR THE HOMELAND DEFENSE MISSION

Andrew M. Brown
Lieutenant, United States Navy
B.S., United States Naval Academy, 2005.

Submitted in partial fulfillment of the
requirements for the degree of

MASTER OF ARTS IN SECURITY STUDIES
(HOMELAND SECURITY AND DEFENSE)

from the

NAVAL POSTGRADUATE SCHOOL
March 2013

Author: Andrew M. Brown

Approved by: James C. Moltz, Ph.D.
                     Thesis Advisor

                     Wayne Hughes, Captain, USN (Ret.)
                     Second Reader

                     Harold A. Trinkunas, Ph.D.
                     Chair, Department of National Security Affairs

THIS PAGE INTENTIONALLY LEFT BLANK

ABSTRACT

This thesis examines how the composition of the U.S. fleet, with specific focus on small combatants, affects the ability of the United States Navy to undertake homeland defense missions and provides suggestions to improve its core competency.

Currently, the U.S. Navy relies on a shrinking group of aging *Oliver Hazard Perry* class frigates to conduct counter-piracy, counter-narcotics, counter maritime insurgency, and maritime engagement missions. The large warships that make up the rest of the fleet are able to undertake these missions, but their cost and capabilities make them better suited for other operations. This thesis examines the proposed Littoral Combat Ship but argues that it is not the ideal ship: it is too expensive, too vulnerable, and undermanned, and it has a modular concept that is too underdeveloped for practical naval operations. Instead, this thesis proposes that the U.S. Navy would be better served by procuring a traditional frigate or corvette to accomplish the variety of missions that fall under the umbrella of homeland defense. Such a traditional small combatant would provide the U.S. Navy with a warship capable of conducting traditional fleet operations as well as operating at the lower end of the spectrum of operations.

THIS PAGE INTENTIONALLY LEFT BLANK

TABLE OF CONTENTS

I. INTRODUCTION 1
   A. LITERATURE REVIEW 2

II. THE ROLE OF THE NAVY AND THE FLEET 7
   A. MISSION OF THE NAVY 7
   B. HOMELAND DEFENSE 10
      1. The Regions of Homeland Defense 14
      2. Homeland Defense Missions 15
         a. Counter-piracy. 16
         b. Counter-narcotics. 18
         c. Maritime Counter-insurgency 19
         d. Maritime Engagement 21

III. THE FLEET 23
   A. CURRENT FLEET DESIGN 23
   B. CONSIDERATIONS IN CONSTRUCTING A FLEET 25
      1. Type 25
      2. Cost 26

IV. CURRENT FLEET CAPABILITIES 29
   A. OLIVER HAZARD PERRY CLASS 29
   B. LITTORAL COMBAT SHIP (LCS) 31
      1. *Freedom* class 35
      2. *Independence* class 36
      3. Modules 37
         a. SUW Module 38
         b. ASW Module 39
         c. MCM Module 39
   C. CONCLUSION 40

V. CRITIQUES OF CURRENT PLANS 41
   A. FLEET COMPOSITION 41
      1. CNA Report 42
      2. CSBA Report 42
      3. OFT Report 43
   B. LCS 44
      1. Cost 44
      2. Vulnerability 46
      3. Manning 49
      4. Modules 50

VI. ALTERNATE SOLUTIONS 53
   A. ALTERNATE FORCE STRUCTURE 54
   B. ALTERNATE SHIP TYPES 56
      1. Corvette 56

		a.	Visby class	58
		b.	Eilat (Sa'ar 5) class	60
		c.	Braunschweig (K130) class	62
	2.	Modular Frigate		63
		a.	Absalon class	64
	3.	Patrol frigate		66
		a.	MEKO A-200 SAN class	67
		b.	Legend class	69
C.	CONCLUSION			71
VII.	CONCLUSION			73
	A.	RECOMMENDATIONS		74
	B.	FURTHER RESEARCH		74

LIST OF REFERENCES 77

INITIAL DISTRIBUTION LIST 85

LIST OF FIGURES

Figure 1. USS *De Wert* (FFG-45) (From IHS Jane's, 2012) 29
Figure 2. USS *Freedom* (LCS-1) (From IHS Jane's, 2012) 35
Figure 3. USS *Independence* (LCS-2) (From IHS Jane's, 2012) 36
Figure 4. *HMS Helsingborg* (K32) (From IHS Jane's, 2011).. 58
Figure 5. *INS Hanit* (503) (From IHS Jane's, 2012)... 60
Figure 6. FGS *Magdeburg* (F-261) (From IHS Jane's, 2012) 62
Figure 7. HDMS *Absalon* (L16) (From IHS Jane's, 2012).. 64
Figure 8. SAS *Isandlwana* (F146) (From IHS Jane's, 2012) 67
Figure 9. USCG *Bertholf* (WMSL-750) (From IHS Jane's, 2012)...................................... 69

THIS PAGE INTENTIONALLY LEFT BLANK

LIST OF ACRONYMS AND ABBREVIATIONS

ALMDS	Airborne Laser Mine Detection System
ARG	Amphibious Ready Group
ASCM	Anti-Ship Cruise Missile
ASW	Antisubmarine Warfare
CG	Cruiser, Guided Missile
CJCS	Chairman of the Joint Chiefs of Staff
CNA	Center for Naval Analyses
CNO	Chief of Naval Operations
CONOPS	Concept of Operations
CODAG	Combined Diesel and Gas
CODOG	Combined Diesel or Gas
CRS	Congressional Research Service
CS	Civil Support
CSBA	Center for Strategic and Budgetary Analysis
CSG	Carrier Strike Group
CVN	Aircraft Carrier, Nuclear Powered
DDG	Destroyer, Guided Missile
DoD	Department of Defense
EP	Emergency Preparedness
FFG	Frigate, Guided Missile
GAO	Government Accountability Office
HA/DR	Humanitarian Assistance/Disaster Relief
HD	Homeland Defense
HS	Homeland Security
JP	Joint Publication
LCS	Littoral Combat Ship
LHA	Amphibious Assault Ship, General Purpose
LHD	Amphibious Assault Ship, Multipurpose
LPD	Amphibious Transport Ship, Dock

LSD	Dock Landing Ship
MCM	Mine Countermeasures
MFTA	Multi-Function Towed Array
MM	Mission Module
MP	Mission Package
MS	Mission System
NLOS-LS	Non-Line of Sight Launch System
NSC	National Security Cutter
NVR	Naval Vessel Rules
OFT	Office of Force Transformation
OHP	Oliver Hazard Perry
SAM	Surface to Air Missile
SSN	Submarine, Nuclear Powered
SUW	Antisurface Warfare
UAV	Unmanned Aerial Vehicle
USV	Unmanned Surface Vehicle
UUV	Unmanned Underwater Vehicle
VDS	Variable Depth Sonar
VLS	Vertical Launch System

ACKNOWLEDGMENTS

I would like to thank both of my advisors for their help and support throughout my writing process. I want to thank James C. Moltz, Ph.D., my thesis advisor, for his advice and guidance on my topic. I am especially grateful that he allowed me to work at my own pace and helped me to refocus my efforts when my topic became too broad. I also want to thank Captain Wayne Hughes, USN (Ret), my second reader, for his counsel and opinions on the future of the Navy. The articles he provided me were essential to the strong foundation of my thesis. Last, I would like to thank my family, for without them and their support, I never would have made it through graduate school.

THIS PAGE INTENTIONALLY LEFT BLANK

I.   INTRODUCTION

The concept of homeland defense is not new; the Navy has always played a crucial role in keeping the threat far from the shores of the United States. However, the changing maritime security environment over the last decade has required that the Navy reevaluate its mission priorities. The modern Navy now plays a substantial role in non-traditional missions like counter narcotics, counter proliferation, counter piracy, and engagement and training with foreign navies. The role of the Navy has shifted away from the traditional Mahanian concept of the blue water fleet and toward the littoral regions with actions against smaller navies and non-state actors that pose different threats to the United States. The Navy has not abandoned blue water operations, but now the increasing importance of the littorals has forced a change. As such, the homeland defense mission of the Navy has become much more important.

The purpose of this thesis is to examine the composition of the U.S. fleet, with specific focus on the small combatants, in order to evaluate fleet composition affects the ability of the United States Navy to undertake the various homeland defense missions. Additionally, this thesis seeks to provide suggestions to improve this core competency of the Navy. This thesis will address a number of questions concerning the composition of the fleet. The first question that must be answered is: Is the current fleet adequate or optimal for the homeland defense mission? The second question is: If the fleet is not adequately or optimally designed to handle the homeland defense mission, what capabilities are lacking? The third question that must be answered is: What would be the optimum way of adding these capabilities to the fleet?

Historically, Navy ships followed along the traditional methods of employment and operation and were designed with a specific purpose in mind and a specific role within the fleet, ranging from air defense to anti-submarine warfare to shore bombardment. These ships were capable of conducting multiple missions, but specialized in doing one mission very well. But changes in tactics and technology have increasingly led to the Navy developing general-purpose ships, such as the Alreigh Burke (DDG-51) class, and developing new classes of ships, such as the Littoral Combat Ship

1

(LCS-1 and LCS-2) classes, which are modular and can be reconfigured for a variety of missions, depending on what equipment is installed.[1]

Currently, the fleet may not be optimally designed to undertake many homeland defense and security missions. Utilizing sophisticated ships that are designed to conduct air defense operations around to strike group in conduct counter-piracy, counter-narcotics, and other missions outside the traditional realm of fleet operations is a waste of resources. A number of the missions that fall under the definition of homeland defense occur in the littoral regions where the Navy is unaccustomed and ill equipped to operate. The current fleet is still composed of the same types of ships needed to defeat a blue water threat during the Cold War. Although almost any Navy ship can handle these non-traditional missions in some form or another, it is a waste of resources for a ship designed around one of the most advanced air-search radar and weapons systems to be conducting these missions. Instead, the Navy may need to construct small, inexpensive types of vessels, like corvettes or frigates, which could handle a number of tasks as part of the homeland defense mission while still being able to operate with the fleet during times of traditional war at sea.

A.   LITERATURE REVIEW

There is a fair amount of literature available concerning the current and future capabilities of the Navy. A number of sources of information come from official Department of Defense and Department of the Navy publications and provide the official definition of the homeland defense mission. The most important of these, the *Naval Operations Concept*, is designed to provide a united vision for the three maritime forces (U.S. Navy, U.S. Marine Corps, U.S. Coast Guard) at the strategic level.[2] Written in 2010, the *Naval Operations Concept* provides a unified vision of how the three maritime services will work together in order to enhance the security of the United States.[3]

---

[1] U.S. Library of Congress, Congressional Research Service, *Navy Littoral Combat Ship (LCS) Program: Background, Issues, and Options for Congress,* by Ronald O'Rourke, CRS Report RL33741, (Washington, DC: Office of Congressional Information and Publishing, December 21, 2012), 1–2.

[2] U.S. Navy, U.S. Marine Corps, U.S. Coast Guard, *Naval Operations Concept 2010: Implementing the Maritime Strategy* (Washington, DC: 2010), 1.

[3] *Naval Operations Concept 2010,* 1–4.

Like the *Naval Operations Concept*, the 2007 *A Cooperative Strategy for 21st Century Seapower* serves to unite the three maritime services at the strategic and operational level.[4] Both Joint Publication (JP) 3-27 *Homeland Defense* and Joint Publication (JP) 3-28 *Civil Support* provide additional strategic information concerning the many roles of the Navy in the these missions.[5] All four official sources provide excellent insight into the official view on the role of the Navy in the homeland defense mission.

In addition to the Department of Defense and Department of Navy publications, the largest volume of information comes from a number of Congressional Research Service reports (CRS). The most important of the CRS reports are the Background, Issues, and Options for Congress reports concerning the Littoral Combat Ship (LCS). The *Navy Littoral Combat Ship (LCS) Program: Background, Issues, and Options for Congress* report covers a number of pressing issues relating to both the LCS-1 and LCS-2 classes of ships. Specifically, the report addresses the numerous problems with construction, corrosion, cost overruns, and problems with the mission modules.[6]

The final CRS report, the *Coast Guard Cutter Procurement: Background and Issues for Congress*, looks at the entirety of the Coast Guard's procurement program, and the construction of the new National Security Cutter (NSC), Offshore Patrol Cutters, and Fast Response Cutters. The report provides an overview of all three programs, the missions of each class of ship, and elaborates on the procurement and construction problems that the NSC has faced.[7]

---

[4] U.S. Navy, U.S. Marine Corps, U.S. Coast Guard, *A Cooperative Strategy for 21st Century Seapower* (Washington, DC: Department of Defense, October 2007), 4–5.

[5] U.S. Office of the Chairman of the Joint Chiefs of Staff, *Homeland Defense Joint Publication (JP) 3-27*, (Washington, DC: CJCS, 12 July 2007); U.S. Office of the Chairman of the Joint Chiefs of Staff, *Civil Support Joint Publication (JP) 3-28*, (Washington, DC: CJCS, September 14 ,2007).

[6] CRS, *Navy Littoral Combat Ship*, 1-6; CRS, *Navy Littoral Combat Ship*, 16; CRS, *Navy Littoral Combat Ship*, 36–37.

[7] U.S. Library of Congress, Congressional Research Service, *Coast Guard Cutter Procurement: Background and Issues for Congress,* by Ronald O'Rourke, CRS Report RL33753, (Washington, DC: Office of Congressional Information and Publishing, July 31, 2012), 2–3.

Only one CRS report examines alternate fleet compositions. In 2007, the CRS issued *Navy Force Structure: Alternative Force Structure Studies of 2005—Background for Congress*. This report summarizes three different reports from 2005 by the Center for Naval Analyses (CNA), the Office of Force Transformation (OFT), and the Center for Strategic and Budgetary Analysis (CSBA).[8] Both the CNA and OFT are Department of Defense organizations, while the CSBA is an independent group. Both the CNA and CSBA reports describe a fleet very similar to the official Navy shipbuilding plan. The OFT report, however, creates three possible fleets, two of those fleets are radically different from anything the Navy has ever built.[9]

Another source of official information comes from the Government Accountability Office (GAO). Like the CRS reports, the GAO report covers the LCS program. And like the CRS reports, the GAO reports are critical of the programs, yet still officially support the continued acquisition of the LCS. The two GAO reports on the LCS program, *Actions Needed to Improve Operating Cost Estimates and Mitigating Risk in Implementing New Concepts* and *Navy's Ability to Overcome Challenges Facing the Littoral Combat Ship Will Determine Eventual Capabilities*, show that the LCS program relies too heavily on unproven technologies and concepts and serious thought needs to be done before the ships enter the fleet.[10]

The final official source comes from the Congressional Budget Office (CBO). In 2009, the CBO published a paper looking at the possible benefits of combining the Navy (LCS) and Coast Guard (NSC) small combatant programs.[11] The CBO report examines three different possibilities on combining the Coast Guard NSC and OPC programs and

---

[8] U.S. Library of Congress, Congressional Research Service, *Navy Force Structures: Alternative Force Structures Studies of 2005—Background for Congress,* by Ronald O'Rourke, CRS Report RL33955, (Washington, DC: Office of Congressional Information and Publishing, April 9, 2007.

[9] CRS, *Navy Force Structures,* 5.

[10] U.S. Government Accountability Office, *Actions Needed to Improve Operating Cost Estimates and Mitigating Risks in Implementing New Concepts, GAO-10-257,* (Washington, DC: Government Printing Office, 2010), 1; U.S Government Accountability Office, *Navy's Ability to Overcome Challenges Facing the Littoral Combat Ship Will Determine Eventual Capabilities, GAO-10-523* (Washington, DC: Government Printing Office, 2010), 1.

[11] Congressional Budget Office, *Options for Combining the Navy's and the Coast Guard's Small Combatant Programs* (Washington, DC: GPO, 2009), 1.

Navy LCS programs: 1) base the NSC on a variant of the LCS; 2) reduce the number of LCSs purchased by the Navy and have the Navy purchase a version of the NSC; or 3) cancel the OPC and have the Coast Guard purchase additional NSCs. The report finds that though there are some benefits with merging the two programs, additional work would be required to satisfy the requirements of both services.[12]

Though the CRS and GAO reports concerning the LCS program are critical of certain aspects of the program, they all agree that the Navy has made the correct decision. The most critical voices come from outside the Department of Defense (DoD) and the Department of the Navy, specifically from naval officers and defense industry officials. A number of critical articles have been written for the U.S. Naval Institute magazine concerning the LCS program. In the April 2012 issue of *Proceedings* magazine, Lieutenant Commander Chuck Schlise, USN, wrote an article about the Navy's need to create a class of ships to fit in the gap between the low end LCS and the high end DDG-51.[13] In another *Proceedings* article, Lieutenant Colonel Paul T. Darling, Alaska Army National Guard, and Lieutenant Justin Lawlor, USNR, wrote an article detailing the need for a frigate-like vessel with multi-mission capabilities, instead of the LCS.[14] In January 2011, U.S. Navy (Ret.) Commander John Patch wrote an article for *Proceedings* magazine enumerating the problems with the LCS program.[15] He criticizes the program for its complexity, cost, impractically, inefficiency, vulnerability and risk, and provides a number of options for fixing the program or replacing it.[16] Milan Vego wrote in the September 2009 issue of *Proceedings* an article discussing a number of flaws in the LCS program. According to Vego, the greatest flaw with the LCS platform is the emphasis on speed at the expense of weapons systems and survivability.[17] In September 2012, U.S. Navy (Ret.) Captain Robert Carney Powers wrote an article that details the history of the

---

[12] CBO, *Small Combatants*, 14–20.

[13] Chuck Schlise, "Shooting for the Middle," *Proceedings*, April 2012, accessed February 21, 2013, http://www.usni.org/print/23988.

[14] Paul T Darling and Justin Lawlor, "Frigates for Streetfighters," *Proceedings*, September 2011, accessed February 21, 2013, http://www.usni.org/magazines/proceedings/2011-09/frigates-streetfighters.

[15] John Patch, "The Wrong Ship at the Wrong Time," *Proceedings*, January 2011, accessed February 21, 2013, http://www.usni.org/magazines/proceedings/2011-01/wrong-ship-wrong-time.

[16] Patch, "Wrong Ship, Wrong Time."

[17] Milan Vego, "No Need for High Speed," *Proceedings*, September 2009, accessed February 21, 2013 http://www.usni.org/magazines/proceedings/2009-09/no-need-high-speed.

LCS program and looks at how both versions of the LCS have diverged from the original intention of the ship.[18]

But not all of the *Proceedings* articles are critical of the LCS program. In June 2012, Edward Walsh wrote an article detailing a number of positive reports concerning the LCS program. According to the article, the Navy is aware of the problems with the LCS program and the majority of the identified problems have already been addressed.[19]

Another contradictory viewpoint comes from Patrick H. Stadt, an executive at Huntington-Ingalls Industries, who argues that the Navy should purchase a version of the Coast Guard NSC to fill the gaps left by the LCS in certain missions.[20] Because Stadt's company stands to build these ships, his objectivity is questionable.[21]

The most important dissenting view comes from a study chaired by U.S. Navy (Ret). Captain Wayne P. Hughes called *The New Navy Fighting Machine: A Study of the Connections between Contemporary Policy, Strategy, Sea Power, Naval Operations, and the Composition of the United States Fleet*.[22] Hughes argues that the Navy needs to create a special class of ships designed exclusively for combat in the littoral regions. Specifically, Hughes calls for the creation of what he calls a "coastal combat flotilla" comprised of small, heavily armed ships and large support vessels to be used to handle combat close to shore and other irregular missions.[23]

---

[18] Robert Carney Powers, "Birth of the Littoral Combat Ship," *Proceedings*, September 2012, accessed February 21, 2013, http://www.usni.org//magazines/proceedings/2012-09-0/birth-littoral-combat-ship.

[19] Edward J Walsh, "Naval Systems-Navy Disputes LCS Criticisms," *Proceedings*, June 2012, accessed February 21, 2013, http://www.usni.org/magazines/proceedings/2012-06/naval-systems-navy-disputes-lcs-criticisms, accessed.

[20] Patrick H Stadt, "Industry View: Why the Navy needs a "Patrol Frigate," *DoD Buzz*, accessed February 21, 2013, http://www.dodbuzz.com/2012/03/28/industry-view-why-the-navy-needs-a-patrol-frigate/.

[21] Patrick H. Stadt works as the corporate director of customer relations for Huntington-Ingalls Industries, the company responsible for the construction of the National Security Cutter.

[22] Wayne P. Hughes, Jr., "The New Navy Fighting Machine: A Study of the Connections Between Contemporary Policy, Strategy, Sea Power, Naval Operations, and the Composition of the United States Fleet," (NPS Study NPSOR-09-002-PR, Naval Postgraduate School, 2009).

[23] Ibid, 19.

II. THE ROLE OF THE NAVY AND THE FLEET

A. MISSION OF THE NAVY

In October 2007, the Navy released a new strategic document titled *A Cooperative Strategy for 21st Century Seapower*, which outline the missions and capabilities of the Navy. According to this document, the mission of the Navy can be described in six strategic imperatives and the six core competencies that are derived from them. The six strategic imperatives for the United States Navy are:

- Limit regional conflict with forward deployed, decisive maritime powers
- Deter major power war
- Win our nation's wars
- Contribute to homeland defense in depth
- Foster and sustain cooperative relationships with more international partners
- Prevent or contain local disruptions before they impact the global system.[24]

The six strategic imperatives are used to develop the core capacities that the Navy must maintain proficiency in. These capabilities are:

- Forward presence
- Deterrence
- Sea control
- Power projection
- Maritime security
- Humanitarian assistance and disaster response.[25]

The Navy maintains forward presence around the world through a combination of forward stationed forces and rotationally deployed forces.[26] Forward stationed forces consist of the various naval units that are permanently based outside of the United States with the purpose of providing continuous naval presence in high-tension areas. The

---

[24] *A Cooperative Strategy for 21st Century Seapower*, 9–11.

[25] Ibid., 12–14.

[26] *2010 Naval Operations Concept*, 26.

rotationally deployed forces consist of vessels homeported within the United States that deploy overseas on a rotating schedule. The mixture of the forward deployed and rotationally deployed forces allows the Navy to maintain a worldwide presence to handle the entire spectrum of operations simultaneously. But this system is not perfect. There are benefits and drawbacks attached to having ships forward deployed or rotationally deployed. Forward deployed ships have the advantage of location over the ships based in the United States. Drawbacks of forward deployed ships include the requirement of significant support from the host nation for basing and increased ship maintenance periods due to extended operational commitments. Rotationally deployed forces do not require extensive facilities overseas to support their operations, but the number of ships required to maintain an overseas presence is increased greatly due to the time required to maintain, train, and deploy a ship from the United States to where it is needed.[27]

The deterrence missions, both nuclear and conventional, have been one of the Navy's more important roles.[28] The nuclear deterrent power of the Navy lies in its ability to deliver a second strike in the event of a nuclear attack on the United States. The conventional deterrent power of the Navy lies in its ability to use conventional forces and weaponry to strike anywhere in the world. But recent events have required a reexamining of the nature of deterrence; no longer does the Navy only have to worry about deterring aggression on the part of state actors. Now the Navy must ensure that it is able to deter aggression on the part of nonstate actors in addition to the traditional state actors.

Sea control is another of the most essential and traditional missions of the United States Navy; without it, the Navy would not be able to operate globally with near impunity.[29] The Navy defines sea control as, "the employment of naval forces, supported by land and air forces as appropriate, in order to achieve military objectives in vital sea areas."[30] Sea control has traditionally translated to the ability of the Navy to find and

---

[27] Ibid.

[28] Ibid., 73.

[29] Ibid., 51.

[30] Ibid., 52.

destroy the enemy's fleet, while protecting its own. During the Cold War, this was straightforward. Cold War-era sea control was based on the ability of the Navy to track Soviet submarines and surface ships and limit their ability to operated freely at sea. But modern adversaries are not investing in traditional fleets. Instead, they investing in new types of diesel submarines, heavily armed surface ships, land-based anti-ship missiles, ballistic anti-ship missiles, and fast attack craft. As such, the sea control mission has evolved from denying the use of the sea to the enemy and into enforcing freedom of navigation and conducting antipiracy patrols, while at the same time maintaining the ability to destroy the enemy's fleet.[31]

Another mission of the Navy is power projection. The Navy is able to directly project power from the sea onto land, either through the use of aircraft or through the use of guided missiles.[32] The Navy is able to conduct strikes through the use of surface, submarine and air-launched weaponry. Additionally, the Navy can project power by utilizing the amphibious capability of the Marine Corps.[33]

Like sea control, maritime security has an essential mission of the U.S. Navy. The United States is, at its heart, a maritime nation and as such depends heavily on the sea for its prosperity and constantly works to ensure that the oceans are secure.[34] The *2010 Naval Operations Concept* defines maritime security as "tasks and operations conducted to protect sovereignty and maritime resources, support free and open seaborne commerce, and to counter maritime related terrorism, weapons proliferation, transnational crime, piracy, environmental destruction, and illegal seaborne immigration."[35] But maritime security is more than just the actions of a single nation; the combined action of many nations working to improve their own maritime security improves the collective maritime security of all nations. Individual maritime security consists of the actions undertaken by a single nation to provide for the safety and security

---

[31] Ibid., 53.

[32] Ibid., 60.

[33] Ibid., 70.

[34] Ibid., 35.

[35] Ibid., 35.

of its own ships and resources at sea. Collective maritime security is the result of the combined actions of many nations to ensure that the oceans are safe for all nations to use. The U.S. Navy conducts a number of engagement and training missions with nations around the world to improve those nations' ability to enforce maritime norms and laws.[36]

The newest competency of the Navy is humanitarian assistance and disaster response (HA/DR). Though HA/DR is not a traditional use of naval assets, the ships of the Navy are uniquely suited to this role and it has become one of the most common uses of naval assets. From 1970 to 2000, the forces of the United States were involved in 366 humanitarian missions compared to only 22 combat missions.[37] Unlike other parts of the government, the Navy does not have to rely on ports and airfields in nations affected by disasters. Navy ships have their own organic aviation lift assets, and amphibious assets are able to move people and goods from ship to shore without host nation port facilities. The HA/DR missions include support to civil authorities, humanitarian assistance, disaster relief, foreign assistance, humanitarian assistance, development assistance, environmental response operations, and security assistance. HA/DR missions can be both reactive and proactive. Reactive HA/DR occurs after a natural disaster, while proactive HA/DR works to strengthen host nation capabilities to recover from disasters before they occur.[38]

B.   HOMELAND DEFENSE

Each of the core competencies is directly involved with the homeland defense (HD) imperative of the Navy to some extent. Probably the most obvious are the deterrence, sea control, power projection, and forward presence missions. Each of these missions works toward to preventing attacks on the U.S. homeland. The less obvious are the effects of maritime security and HA/DR on homeland defense. Both maritime security and HA/DR missions work to build the capacities of other nations around the world to protect their own interests. And by improving the capabilities of these nations to

---

[36] Ibid., 41.

[37] Ibid., 46.

[38] Ibid., 45–48.

handle internal issues like terrorism, proliferation, smuggling, and narcotics, the overall security of the United States improves. By building up the capabilities of those nations less equipped to handle those issues, the United States is able to positively affect the homeland defense mission.

In order to understand the role of the Navy in the HD mission, three concepts must be made clear. The first of these concepts is the homeland and its size. The official definition of the homeland is the "physical region that includes the continental United States, Alaska, Hawaii, U.S. territories and possessions, and surrounding territorial waters and airspace."[39] The United States covers an area of 3,794,100 square miles, has land boundaries of 7,478 miles, and 12,380 miles of coastline, which makes the United States the third largest territory in the world.[40] This does not cover the area of the sixteen additional territories and possessions of the United States.[41] The second concept of HD is that the homeland is vulnerable. The U.S. government believes that the homeland is "is exposed to the possibility of harm from hostile states or non-state actors" and as such must be protected from outside attack.[42] It is the role of the Department of Defense to ensure that threats are met and handled well before they reach the United States.[43] And as the primary instrument of national security, it falls on the military to protect the homeland. The Department of Defense is the primary agent for homeland defense.[44] The third concept of HD is that HD is different from homeland security (HS). HS is focused internally, while HD has an external focus. The role of HS is to protect the United States

---

[39] CJCS, *JP 3-27*, I-1.

[40] Central Intelligence Agency, *CIA World Factbook: United States*, accessed February 12, 2013, https://www.cia.gov/library/publications/the-world-factbook/geos/us.html; Central Intelligence Agency, *CIA World Factbook: Country Comparison::Areas*, accessed February 12, 2013, https://www.cia.gov/library/publications/the-world-factbook/rankorder/2147rank.html?countryName=United%20States&countryCode=us&regionCode=noa&rank=3#us.

[41] The government of the United States administers sixteen different territories as insular areas. These territories are: American Samoa, Guam, the Northern Mariana Islands, Puerto Rico, the U.S. Virgin Islands, the Bajo Nuevo Bank, Baker Island, Howland Island, Jarvis Island, Johnston Atoll, Kingman Reef, Midway Island, Navassa Island, Palmyra Atoll, Serranilla Bank, and Wake Island.

[42] CJCS, *JP 3-27*, I-1.

[43] Ibid., I-6.

[44] Ibid., I-2; "About the Department of Defense," accessed February 7, 2013, http://www.defense.gov/about/#mission,.

from attacks originating from within. The 2007 *National Security Strategy for Homeland Security* defines homeland security as, "a concerted national effort to prevent terrorist attacks within the United States, reduce America's vulnerability to terrorism, and minimize the damage from and recover from attacks that do occur."[45] HS missions can occur simultaneously across all levels of government, from the local, tribal, state, or federal levels. JP 3-27, *Homeland Defense*, defines homeland defense as the "protection of U.S. sovereignty, territory, domestic population, and critical defense infrastructure against external threats and aggression, or other threats as directed by the President." [46] Because HD missions deal with external threats to the sovereignty of the United States, they only occur at the national level.

The variety of HD missions can further be broken down into three categories: traditional, civil support, or emergency preparedness. The traditional HD mission involves projecting national power in order to deter, prevent, or disrupt an attack against the United States.[47] Civil support (CS) missions are the use of traditional military capabilities providing either assistance to domestic and foreign governments or law enforcement agencies.[48] The *Strategy for Homeland Defense and Civil Support* defines CS as, "DoD support, including Federal military forces, the Department's career civilian and contractor personnel, and DoD agency and component assets, for domestic emergencies and for designated law enforcement and other activities."[49] Even though CS missions fall under HD, the DoD is legally restricted to a supporting role by the 1878 *Posse Comitatus Act*.[50] DoD assets may operate in the CS role, but require specific Congressional authorization to do so. These missions may range from responding to a

---

[45] Department of Defense, *National Strategy for Homeland Security*, (Washington, DC: Government Printing Office, October 2007), 3.

[46] CJCS, *JP 3-27*, I-1.

[47] Department of Defense, *Strategy for Homeland Defense and Civil Support*, (Washington, DC: Government Printing Office, June 2005), 10.

[48] CJCS, *JP 3-28 Civil Support*, I-1.

[49] DoD, *Strategy for Homeland Defense and Civil Support*, 5–6.

[50] U.S. Government Accountability Office, *DOD Can Enhance Efforts to Identify Capabilities to Support Civil Authorities during Disasters GAO-03-670* (Washington, DC: Government Printing Office, March, 2010), 11.

major disaster, restoring order during a civil disturbance, responding to a chemical, biological, radiological, or nuclear incident, and providing support for national special events.[51] Congressional authorization to operate domestically has been granted to the DoD for participating in drug interdiction and certain law enforcement missions, protecting of civil rights, suppressing insurrection, assisting the U.S. Secret Service, protecting nuclear materials, assisting with the response to terrorist incidents involving weapons of mass destruction, and executing and enforcing of quarantine.[52] The emergency preparedness (EP) responsibility of the DoD consists of any and all measures undertaken before a disaster meant to mitigate the loss or damage to life, property, or national institutions.[53] Most importantly, the DoD does not consider EP a separate mission set. The EP exists as a constant state of preparedness that results from the preparation for the DoD's HD and CS role.[54]

The DoD has identified eight mission types that fall under the umbrella of HD and CS and all of them are well suited to naval assets. These eight missions are: identify the threat, deter our enemies from courses of action which may pose a threat to the United States, defend the homeland and deny the enemy's access to the United States airspace, territory, and territorial seas, ensure access to space and information, protect defense critical infrastructure, deter aggression through global operations, defeat the enemy when deterrence fails, and recover from any attack or incident.[55] A number of these missions are identical to the missions of the Navy. The Navy's deterrence mission is directly linked to the HD deterrence mission. The sea control mission of the Navy is directly linked to ensuring access to space and information. The forward presence mission of the Navy serves as both a deterrent and method of access denial. The power projection capability enhances the ability of the nation to defeat their enemies.

---

[51] U.S. Government Accountability Office, *DOD Needs to Address Gaps in Homeland Defense and Civil Support Guidance, GAO-13-128* (Washington, DC: Government Printing Office, October, 2012), 3–4.

[52] GAO, *DOD Can Enhance Efforts to Identify Capabilities to Support Civil Authorities during Disasters*, 11.

[53] CJCS, *JP 3-28*, I-1.

[54] CJCS, *JP 3-27*, I-6.

[55] Ibid., I-3.

1. The Regions of Homeland Defense

In order to protect the homeland, the U.S. government has conceptually divided the world into three distinct regions, based partially on geography, partially on the capabilities of the Navy and the Coast Guard, and partially based the expected capabilities of the enemy.[56] These three regions are the homeland, the approaches, and the forward regions.

The first region is the homeland, which consists of the United States and its territorial waters and airspace. The military is specifically prohibited from operating in anything more than a supporting role by the 1878 *Posse Comitatus Act*.[57] Only agencies with law enforcement responsibilities are allowed to operate in this region in a supervisory role. DoD assets are required to play a supporting role in maritime operations in the homeland. The DoD has a number of missions in this region which include deterring and defeating direct attacks against the United States, supporting civil authorities and law enforcement personnel in support of counterterror operations as directed by the president, and providing chemical, biological, radiological, nuclear, and explosives consequence management support to civilian authorities.[58]

The next region, the approaches, consists of the land, water, and airspace around the United States through which all traffic enters the homeland and extends out to international waters and airspace.[59] Forces in this region are responsible for locating threats before they reach the homeland and defeating them, if necessary.[60] This region is one of blended control and operations. Because the law limits the ability of the DoD to operate in a law enforcement capacity, Navy ships are required to take on a Coast Guard law enforcement detachment while conducting operations in the approaches. In the approaches, the Navy conducts operations in support of the War on Drugs, monitors and

---

[56] Ibid., I-5.

[57] Chairman of the Joint Chiefs of Staff, *Joint Publication 3-26 Homeland Security*, (August 2 ,2005), I-4.

[58] DoD, *Strategy for Homeland Defense and Civil Support*, 12.

[59] Ibid, 11; CJCS, *JP 3-27*, I-5.

[60] CJCS, *JP 3-27*, I-5 – I-6.

14

interdicts suspected smugglers with the support of the Coast Guard, as well as conducts normal maritime military operations.

The third layer is the forward regions. The forward regions consist of all foreign territory, airspace, and waterspace.[61] The role of the military in the forward regions is to project power and deter, detect, prevent attacks, and destroy any and all threats to the homeland.[62] Military operations in this region can occur simultaneously across the entire range of military operations, from engagement and national building operations all the way to direct action missions and global strikes.[63] Unlike the homeland and the approaches, the Navy takes the lead as the primary agent for maritime operations in this region.

Dividing the oceans allows for the government to divide the responsibility of each region between the various Services and Agencies. Ideally, the U.S. Navy takes charge of the efforts in the furthest regions from the homeland and leaves the protecting of the homeland to the Coast Guard. But the sheer size of the problem combined with the limited assets available to the Coast Guard and blended nature of the approaches means that the Navy cannot ignore the HD mission.

2.   Homeland Defense Missions

The addition of the non-traditional homeland defense missions to the traditional missions of the Navy has forced the service to address a number of new missions. The environment that the Navy finds itself in—the post-Cold War period—is full of nontraditional threats. The Navy has been forced to evolve by assuming a number of nontraditional roles. in order to counter these threats. The Navy must now conduct a number of new missions, such as counter-piracy, counternarcotic, maritime security and engagement. It is not cost effective to send a modern destroyer or cruiser on these low threat missions; their capabilities are better utilized on their primary warfare areas. The ideal ships for the HD missions are frigates or corvettes, which have the small size that

---

[61] DoD, *Strategy for Homeland Defense and Civil Support*, 11.

[62] CJCS, *JP 3-27*, I-5.

[63] Ibid., I-5.

allows them to work with and train local forces without overwhelming them and the offensive capabilities to operate as a part of traditional, large-scale naval operations as needed.

a. Counter-piracy.

Piracy is one of the oldest crimes and has existed for thousands of years. But for most of modern history, piracy has been a nuisance rather than a concern. During the latter part of the 1990s pirate activity began to climb around the world, especially in the Straits of Malacca and off of the Horn of Africa. Between 2000 and 2009, there were approximately 3500 incidents of maritime piracy, with only 16 percent of those attacks occurring off of Africa.[64] Due to increased presence off the Horn of Africa, piracy in that area has declined somewhat, but has increased in the Gulf of Guinea off the Atlantic coast of the continent.

Piracy is a general term used to describe three different types of crimes at sea. One type is the robbery of ships while in port. Pirates in this kind of attack are normally after cash and small, high-value items that can be removed quickly.[65] Another type of piracy is attacks against ships on the open seas with the intent of holding the ships, crew, and cargo for ransom.[66] A third type of piracy consists of vessels being hijacked with the express purpose of stealing both the ship and cargo, giving the ship a fake registration, taking on a fresh cargo, and then stealing the new cargo. These vessels tend to be the smaller freighters used to take cargo regionally, rather than transoceanic. These ships are continuously given fake names and registrations until they are captured or abandoned.[67] Of these three types of attacks, only the second is of major concern to the world. The pirating of an oil tanker or bulk cargo carrier could have worldwide

---

[64] United Nations Office on Drugs and Crime (UNODC), *The Globalization of Crime: A Transnational Organized Crime Threat Assessment* (Vienna, Austria: United Nations, 2010), 193.

[65] Peter Chalk*, The Maritime Dimension of International Security: Terrorism, Piracy, and Challenges for the United States* (Santa Monica, California: Rand, 2008), 5.

[66] Ibid.

[67] Ibid., 6.

economic and political implications. The first and third categories of piracy are a criminal nuisance, but their impact is negligible.

It is difficult to accurately describe the impact of piracy on the international economy; shipping companies make incomplete reports of attempted acts of piracy for fear of increased insurance premiums or ships being stuck in port while investigations happen. It is estimated that less than 50 percent of pirate attacks are reported to the International Maritime Bureau.[68] With the average pirated vessel fetching from $500,000 to $2 million in ransom, it is estimated that piracy costs the world somewhere from $1 billion to $16 billion per year.[69] But the cost of piracy is more than just monetary. Piracy undermines legitimate governments and the ransoms serve to prop up illegitimate governments. Piracy is one of the few missions of the military that is explicitly described in the Constitution and one of the oldest missions of the U.S. Navy. Section 8 of Article 1 of the U.S. Constitution gives Congress the power to, "To define and punish Piracies and Felonies committed on the high Seas, and Offences against the Law of Nations."[70] Some of the first missions of the Navy were raids against the pirates operating out of what is modern-day Libya. More recently, the Navy has found itself again participating in widespread counter-piracy operations around the world, but specifically off the Horn of Africa in conjunction with the NATO through Operation OCEAN SHIELD.[71]

There are a number of reasons why piracy is a major concern. Most importantly, the oceans are essential to the world's economy. It is estimated that at any one time there are somewhere between 15 to 16 million containers and as much as 6 billion tons of crude oil and bulk materials on the sea at any one time. Next, many of the most important sea-lanes and maritime chokepoints are located along failed or failing states. These regions create a unique mixture of ships being geographically concentrated

---

[68] Ibid., 7.

[69] Ibid., 16.

[70] U.S. Constitution, Art. I, § 8, cl. 10.

[71] NATO, "Operation Ocean Shield", http://www.aco.nato.int/page208433730.aspx, accessed March 3, 2013.

and slowed down in areas with a lack of international customs enforcement. Pirates in these regions benefit from the weak or failed state governments, often employing bribes and protection to allow pirates to operate. The sheer number of ships transiting the Straits of Malacca, Gulf of Aden, and Bab El-Mandab and the number of small craft in these areas lets the pirates blend in easily in to the background and access to more ships than can possibly be protected. Finally, some attribute the rise in piracy to the worldwide economic recession that occurred in the first part of the 21st Century. Lack of economic opportunities drove people into crime, and piracy is an easy and relatively inexpensive option. The economic downturn in conjunction with the decreased maritime security and the sheer enormity problem has limited the ability of many poorer nations to patrol their own waters.[72]

b. *Counter-narcotics*

Law enforcement in support of the War on Drugs has been a secondary mission of the Navy for decades. Beginning in the 1980s, the Navy began conducting operations in support of the War on Drugs off the coasts of South America and the Caribbean Sea. With as many as four Navy ships, typically frigates but sometimes a destroyer, operating in conjunction with the Coast Guard and other law enforcement agencies, the maritime war on drugs has cost upwards of $20 billion over the past decade alone.[73] Traditionally, smugglers utilized fishing boats and high-speed vessels known as go-fast boats to move drugs. These boats are able to carry approximately three tons of cocaine per trip with a value of about $75 million.[74] But the advanced technology and capabilities of the U.S. military have made it increasingly risky to transport drugs along normal channels. To counter this, the drug smugglers have evolved their tactics to improve their chances of avoiding detection.

---

[72] Chalk, *The Maritime Dimension*, 10–13.

[73] Martha Mendoza, "Military Expands Its Drug War in Latin America," *Navy Times*, February 3, 2013, accessed February 20, 2013, http://www.navytimes.com/news/2013/02/SUNDAYap-us-military-expands-drug-war-in-latin-america-020213/.

[74] "Go-fast' boats slip by anti-drug effort," *The Washington Times*, April 16, 2006, accessed February 20, 2013, http://www.washingtontimes.com/news/2006/apr/16/20060416-112558-2981r/.

18

The drug trafficking organizations have begun constructing vessels specifically designed to be difficult to detect. Known as self-propelled semi-submersibles (SPSS), these vessels represent a revolution in drug smuggling technology. Constructed using a combination of fiberglass and steel, SPSS are designed with a minimum amount of freeboard make visual and radar detection difficult. The SPSS have a crew of four to five people and are able to stay at sea for up ten days. These vessels cost approximately $2 million to construct and are able to carry an average of ten tons of drugs per trip.[75]

Recently, a new type of drug smuggling vessel has been discovered in the jungles of South America. Criminal organizations developed a completely submersible vessel to smuggle drugs. Crewed by four to six men, these narco-subs are able to transport as much as twelve tons of cocaine the entire distance from South America to the United States.[76] These ships are very difficult to detect while they are on the surface due to their low freeboard. But some are also able to completely submerge and remain submerged for more than 18 hours operating on battery power before having to surface and recharge their batteries.[77] With a craft costing about $2 million to build, and the estimated profit from one narco-sub trip at over $250 million, the risks are well worth the rewards.[78]

Though this technology has not been used to smuggle anything but drugs, it is not difficult to imagine a narco-sub being used to transport human cargo, terrorists, or weapons of mass destruction into the United States undetected.

c. *Maritime Counter-insurgency*

Another major threat at sea is the rise of maritime insurgency. Often linked to piracy and weapons and drug smuggling, maritime insurgency is no longer just used to fund and supply operations ashore. Insurgent groups have discovered that the sea

---

[75] Brad Lendon, "Two New Narco Subs Found in Colombia," CNN, accessed February 20, 2013, http://news.blogs.cnn.com/2011/09/27/two-new-narco-subs-found-in-colombia.

[76] Joint Interagency Task Force-South, *Joint Interagency Task Force Fact Sheet: Self-Propelled Semi-Submersible*.

[77] Jim Popkin, "Authorities in Awe of Drug Runners' Jungle-Built, Kevlar-Coated Supersubs," *Wired Magazine*, March 29, 2011, accessed February 20, 2013, http://www.wired.com/magazine/2011/03/ff_drugsub/all/1.

[78] Popkin, "Authorities in Awe."

provides unique opportunities. Insurgent groups have begun operating at sea for the same reasons that pirates and smugglers do – the sea provides almost unlimited mobility, and its enormity makes detection very difficult. Additionally, with the economic vitality of the world dependent on the oceans for trade, attacks at sea can have just as much effect as an attack on a target on land.

Attacks at sea for reasons other than economic gain have been rare. Probably the two most famous are the attack on the USS *Cole* (DDG-67) in October of 2000 and the seizure of the *Achille Lauro* in 1985.[79] But these are far from the only cases of terrorism against ships at sea. In 2002, a small boat rammed and exploded next to the French oil tanker *Limburg* off the coast of Yemen that resulted in the death of one crewmember and the release of 90,000 barrels of oil into the ocean.[80] Another case of maritime terrorism occurred in 2004 when an attack took place on the Iraqi oil terminals in the Persian Gulf. Using speedboats filled with explosives, terrorists attempted to destroy the oil terminals, which would have destabilized the world economy through rising oil prices.[81] In 2004, a bomb set off by a member of the Abu Sayyaf terrorist organization exploded and sank the *Superferry 14* off the coast of the Philippines and killed over 100 people.[82] Finally, the best example or maritime terrorism occurred during the 20-year long Sri Lanka civil war, in which the Liberation Tigers of Tamil Elam formed a sea cadre known as the Sea Tigers. The Sea Tigers conducted multiple raids and attacks against Sri Lankan forces and demonstrated how cheaply and effectively a maritime insurgency can be conducted.[83] The risk of maritime insurgency cannot be understated. The ramifications of a sunken oil tanker or cruise ship would be politically and economically enormous.

---

[79] Martin N. Murphy, "The Unwanted Challenge," *Proceedings Magazine*, http://www.usni.org/magazines/proceedings/2008-12/unwanted-challenge, accessed March 1, 2013.

[80] "Yemen Says Tanker Blast Was Terrorism," BBC News, accessed March 1, 2013, http://news.bbc.co.uk/2/hi/middle_east/2334865.stm.

[81] "Blast Tragets Iraqi Oil Terminals," BBC News, accessed March 1, 2013, http://news.bbc.co.uk/2/hi/middle_east/3656481.stm.

[82] Murphy, "The Unwanted Challenge."

[83] Paul A. Povlock, "The Coming Maritime Insurgent Century," *Proceedings Magazine,* accessed March 1, 2013, http://www.usni.org/magazines/proceedings/2012-12/coming-maritime-insurgent-century.

d. *Maritime Engagement*

The final type of mission associated with HD is maritime engagement. Maritime engagement missions serve to increase the individual maritime security of nations around the world through the training and mentoring of partner-nation naval forces by members of the U.S. Navy. By improving the partner-nation's ability to secure their territorial waters, the U.S. Navy is able to improve collective maritime security around the world. The U.S. Navy provides training to partner-nation forces on seamanship, small boat maintenance, search and rescue, law enforcement and vessel boarding, and maritime law.[84]

One of the largest problems in conducting maritime engagement missions is dealing with the difference between the capabilities of the U.S. Navy vessels and those of the partner-nation. These nations often do not have traditional navies or coast guards and it is important that the training conducted does not go beyond what the partner-nation is capable of.

---

[84] "About Africa Partnership Station," U.S. Navy, www.naveur-navaf.navy.mil\about%20us.html, accessed March 1, 2013.

THIS PAGE INTENTIONALLY LEFT BLANK

III. THE FLEET

In general terms, a fleet can be described in terms of the capabilities that its ships maintain and how those capabilities might be used. Capabilities can be broadly described in four mission areas.[85] The first mission of a navy is to ensure the ability of a nation to move goods and ships freely across the oceans, as well as ensuring the safety of special assets like ballistic missile submarines.[86] The second role of a navy is to deny the enemy the ability to freely use the oceans.[87] The third core function of a navy is the ability to provide goods and services to forces ashore. A navy is required to put a land force ashore to hold territories, as well as provide them with logistical and fire support.[88] The fourth and final competency of a navy is to prevent the enemy from being able to land forces ashore and support them by sea.[89] It is essential that the design of the fleet reflect the missions being done.

A.   CURRENT FLEET DESIGN

The U.S. fleet is designed around two composite structures called the carrier strike group (CSG) and the amphibious ready group (ARG). The CSG and ARG are unique constructs that give the United States significant power projection and strike capabilities around the world without the need for extensive diplomatic clearances and concerns. The Navy can deploy a CSG or ARG off the coast of a nation in order to provide stability or influence events or in preparation to conduct operations. A CSG is normally composed of a single nuclear-powered aircraft carrier (CVN), a carrier air wing, approximately five surface combatants (CG or DDG), one nuclear-powered attack submarine (SSN), and one Military Sealift Command supply ship.[90] The exact number of

---

[85] Wayne P. Hughes, Jr., "Naval Operations: A Close Look at the Operational Level of War at Sea," *Naval War College Review* 65, no. 3, (Summer 2012), 25.

[86] Ibid.

[87] Ibid.

[88] Ibid., 26.

[89] Ibid.

[90] *2010 Naval Operations Concept*, 83; "The Carrier Strike Group," U.S. Navy, http://www.navy.mil/navydata/ships/carriers/powerhouse/cvbg.asp, February 10, 2013.

ships can be increased as mission requirements dictate. The composition and capabilities of the individual units of the CSG allows for it to conduct missions across the entire spectrum of operations, from ballistic missile defense down to maritime security.[91] The Navy currently maintains a 3-2-1 readiness posture for its carrier fleets. This posture requires that three CSGs are deployed, two CVN be ready for deployment within 30 days of notification, and a third CVN ready within 90 days.[92] CSG excel in many of the traditional naval roles but the size and types of ships in a CSG limit their ability to effectively conduct maritime security and HA/DR missions. The complexity of these ships make them inefficient platforms for conducting maritime engagement and their lack of amphibious assets hinder their ability to conduct HA/DR missions.

An ARG normally is composed of one large amphibious assault ship (LHA or LHD), an assortment of amphibious transport dock (LPD) and dock landing ships (LSD), and a SSN. Additionally, an ARG will deploy with one or more surface combatants to provide the air defense, undersea warfare, and strike capabilities.[93] Like the CSG, the ARG is able to project power ashore with its limited strike capabilities; but the majority of the power projection comes from the embarked Marine units and their capabilities. ARGs excel in the forward presence, HA/DR, and amphibious assault roles.[94]

The third component of the fleet is the small combatant ships, such as the minesweepers and the frigates. Frigates (FFG) were designed during the Cold War to provide an antisubmarine warfare capability for amphibious forces, underway replenishment groups and merchant convoys.[95] The FFG in the U.S. Navy have a very limited air defense and anti-surface capability but are very capable in working the non-traditional missions of antipiracy, counter-narcotics, maritime security, and engagement. The minesweepers (MCM) were designed to locate, classify, and destroy both moored

---

[91] Ibid.

[92] *2010 Naval Operations Concept*, 83.

[93] "The Amphibious Ready Group," U.S. Navy, http://www.navy.mil/navydata/nav_legacy.asp?id=148, accessed February 10, 2013.

[94] *2010 Naval Operations Concept*, 85.

[95] "Frigates – FFG," U.S. Navy, http://www.navy.mil/navydata/fact_display.asp?cid=4200&tid=1300&ct=4, accessed February 10, 2013.

and bottom mines.[96] Both the FFG and MCM are no longer in production and are being decommissioned in anticipation of the LCS.

B.   CONSIDERATIONS IN CONSTRUCTING A FLEET

Of all the considerations taken into account when building a fleet, two are the most important: fleet cost and ship capabilities. These two issues need to be factored in when considering the overall missions of those ships.

1.   Type

Two of the most prominent naval strategists, Alfred Thayer Mahan and Julian Corbett, grouped naval units into three categories. These categories are the battle fleet, cruisers, and flotillas.[97] At the center of traditional navies is the battle fleet, which consists of the capital ships and their escorts with the mission of engaging and destroying the enemy's battle fleet for the purpose of winning command of the seas.[98] Traditionally, the battle fleet consisted of battleships and their escorts, but in the modern navy the battle fleet is centered on the aircraft carriers and their battle groups. In the U.S. Navy today, the battle fleet consists of the CSG and the ARG. The second category of naval vessels is what Corbett described as the "cruisers." Cruisers are any vessels designed to locate and attack the enemy's commercial shipping and protect allied shipping. Traditionally, cruisers were lightly armed and armored when compared to battleships, but had significant advantages in range, speed, and unit cost. Originally these vessels were pirates or surface raiders. But since the end of the First World War, these surface combatants have been replaced by submarines, and since the end of the Second World War, the submarines have been augmented with long-range, shore-based anti-ship aircraft and missiles.[99] Corbett believed that a nation couldn't be victorious at sea with only a battle fleet; having a fleet of cruisers was essential to counter enemy raiders or to conduct

---

[96] "Mine Countermeasures Ships – MCM," U.S. Navy, accessed February 10, 2013, http://www.navy.mil/navydata/fact_display.asp?cid=4200&tid=1900&ct=4.

[97] Hughes, "Naval Operations," 27.

[98] Ibid.

[99] Ibid.

a *guerre de course.*[100] *Guerre de course*, or commerce raiding, denies the enemy the ability to operate at sea with impunity, as well as forcing it to divide its battle fleet or risk its commercial shipping. And because of this, Corbett argued that a nation with a strong navy needed to construct a balanced fleet with cruisers to protect its shipping, while at the same time being able to conduct operations against enemy shipping.[101] The third category of ships is the flotilla. According to Corbett, flotillas must be composed of small ships capable of both operating in the littorals that would normally be too hazardous for capital ships and providing escort to the battle fleet and cruisers in hazardous waters. These ships would have a limited range and operational duration, but would have enough firepower like torpedoes and missiles to conduct operations against larger opponents utilizing stealth, surprise, and superior numbers.[102]

2.   Cost

The second consideration in building a fleet is cost. The availability of funding must be taken into account, especially during times of peace when the government has normally cut funding to the military. As ships and systems have become more complex, the cost to build a fleet has increased dramatically. Between 1967 and 2005, the average cost of a guided missile destroyer increased by more than 123 percent, and the cost of a nuclear-powered attack submarine rose by 401 percent.[103] In 1967, the average cost of a guided missile destroyer was $515 million FY 2005 dollars and the average cost of a nuclear-powered attack submarine was $484 FY2005 dollars. By 2005, the average cost of a guided missile destroyer rose to $1.148 billion FY2005 dollars and the cost of a nuclear-powered attack submarine rose to $2.427 FY2005 dollars.[104] There are a number of reasons as to why the cost of the cost of ships has increased but Mark Arena describes them as the economy-driven factors and the customer-driven factors.

---

[100] Ibid.

[101] Ibid.

[102] Ibid.

103 Mark Arena et al., *Why Has the Cost of Navy Ships Risen?* (Santa Monica: Rand National Defense Research Institute, 2006), 2.

104 Ibid.

The first factors, the economy-driven, are the aspects of shipbuilding that are normally outside the influence of the government, such as the cost of labor, materials, and installed equipment.[105] And of those three factors, the majority of the cost comes from the labor and the installed equipment. Between 1977 and 2005, labor costs ran between 30 and 50 percent of the final cost of a ship at U.S. naval shipyards.[106] The most expensive parts of a ship are the pieces of equipment and systems installed on it. The cost of the equipment installed on a Navy warship comprises over 40 percent of its total cost and continues to rise as the cost of technology increases.[107] The material cost of the ship has remained relatively constant and does not make of a significant portion of the overall cost of a ship. On average, the material cost of a ship only composes 15 percent of the final value.[108] Even though these factors compose most of the actual cost of the ship, they are only responsible for half the increase on the cost of a Navy ship.

The second reason for the increasing cost of a warship is the customer-driven factors.[109] Customer-driven factors are those factors determined by the purchaser and can range from the types of systems installed to the number of ships built. The largest component of the Navy customer-driven growth is complexity. Mark Arena defines complexity as the difficulty and level of effort required to plan, construct, and outfit a ship.[110] As any one of those factors increases, the overall complexity of the ship increases and the cost of the warship increases.[111] Additionally, complexity increases as a result of the secondary factors that increase as government priorities change. The traditional factors that affect the capabilities of the warship include the displacement, the number and type of weapon, the amount of armor on the ship, the speed of the ship, and the acquisition cost of the ship.[112] But governmental priorities and regulations have

---

[105] Ibid, 21.

[106] Arena et al., *Why Has the Cost of Navy Ships Risen?*, 24.

[107] Arena et al., *Why Has the Cost of Navy Ships Risen?*, 28.

[108] Ibid., 28.

[109] Ibid., 32.

[110] Ibid.

[111] Ibid.

[112] Ibid.

dictated that factors such as survivability, reaction time, reliability, maintainability, endurance, pollution control, seakeeping, habitability, radar signature, noise signature, sensor range, and total life-cycle cost be taken into account in ship design.[113] Over the last 50 years, changes to these areas have resulted in an unanticipated increase in both the size of the ships and their complexity, which increase the cost of the ship considerably.

Procurement rate and methods also influence the final cost of a warship. The rate at which the ships are procured and the number of locations where the ships are built plays a significant role in determining the final cost of a warship.[114] Higher procurement rates allow for the shipbuilders to scale up their production and drive costs down. Shipyards are more likely to invest in cost-saving measures and efficiency improvements when ships are procured in larger numbers.[115] The incentive to produce ships effectively does not exist at low procurement levels because shipyards need to stretch out production times to stay open. The Navy often utilizes multiple construction yards when procuring new ships in order to keep multiple shipyards operating as a matter of national security and maintaining jobs. The use of multiple yards does have an effect on lowering the cost of the ship and often causes the final cost to increase.[116] With modern weapons and sensor systems driving up the cost of warship construction, it is essential that every effort be made to keep the overall cost of the ship low while still providing the needed capabilities. If the Navy seeks to continue contributing to the HD mission, the Navy needs to work to keep complexity and technology costs to a minimum and create a vessel that can serve as a medium to low-end combatant with existing technologies and designs but sufficient to serve less demanding missions such as offshore patrol and homeland defense.

---

[113] Ibid., 40.

[114] Ibid,, 32; Ibid, 44.

[115] Ibid., 44.

[116] Ibid., 47.

IV. CURRENT FLEET CAPABILITIES

The purpose of this chapter is to describe the current state of medium- to low-end combatants in the U.S. Navy. Currently, the U.S. Navy has no combatant that is designed specifically to operate at this level. The primary platform for HD missions, the *Oliver Hazard Perry* (*OHP*) class frigates, were initially designed as an anti-submarine ship during the Cold War and only began operating as an HD platform when they were no lingered needed in their primary role. To replace these aging ships, the Navy began developing the LCS. The LCS is designed to provide modular combatant capabilities across three different warfare areas. This chapter reviews current and planned capabilities in these small combatants before turning to a critique of Navy plans in Chapter V.

A. OLIVER HAZARD PERRY CLASS

Figure 1. USS *De Wert* (FFG-45) (From IHS Jane's, 2012)

The *OHP* class of frigates was designed at the height of the Cold War to provide open ocean escorts for convoys and amphibious units crossing the Atlantic Ocean in the event of another war in Europe. Since the end of the Cold War, the *OHP* have excelled in the non-traditional realm of homeland defense operations – counter-narcotics, counter-proliferation, counter smuggling, and counter piracy.[117] The Navy initially constructed 51 OHP frigates between 1973 and 1984 at an average cost of $650 million per ship.[118] As of 2013, only 23 of the original OHP are still in service with the U.S. Navy and all should be decommissioned by 2017 and replaced by the LCS.[119]

The OHP have a length of 453.1 feet, a beam of 44.9 feet, a maximum draft of 24.6 feet, and a full load displacement of 4166 tons.[120] The OHP class is powered by two LM2500 gas turbine engines driving a single shaft with two retractable auxiliary propulsion units for slow speed maneuvering.[121] The OHP frigates have a maximum speed of 29 knots and a maximum range of 4500 nautical miles at 20 knots.[122] The OHP frigates are designed for a crew of 15 officers, 200 enlisted personnel, with an additional 19 personnel as part of the aviation detachment.[123]

The OHP class ships are equipped with a Raytheon SPS-49(V)4 or 5 air search radar system, an ISC Cardion SPS-55 surface search radar system, a Sperry Mk 92 fire control radar system, and a Furuno navigation radar.[124] For subsurface search, the *OHP* are equipped with a SQQ 89(V)2 sonar suite, consisting of a Raytheon SWS 56 hull mounted sonar and a Gould SQR 19 passive towed array, allowing them to conduct antisubmarine operations.[125] For defense, the OHP class ships are armed with one OTO Melara 76-millimeter/62 caliber gun system and one General Electric/General Dynamics

---

[117] CBO, *Options for Combining the Navy's and the Coast Guard's Small Combatant Programs*, 5.

[118] CBO, *Options for Combining the Navy's and the Coast Guard's Small Combatant Programs*, 5.

[119] Deputy Chief of Naval Operations (Integration of Capabilities and Resources)(N8), *Annual Report to Congress on Long Range Plan for Construction of Naval Vessels for FY2013*, (Washington, DC: Office of the Chief of Naval Operations, April 2012), 22.

[120] "Oliver Hazard Perry class (FFH)," *IHS Jane's*, April 3, 2012.

[121] Ibid.

[122] Ibid.

[123] Ibid.

[124] Ibid.

[125] Ibid.

20-millimeter Mk 15 1B Vulcan Phalanx gun system.[126] Additionally, two Boeing 25-millimeter Mk 38 guns can be mounted amidships.[127] The OHP class ships were originally armed a single Mk 13 missile launcher with a 40 round missile magazine. The Mk 13 was capable of firing the SM-1MR missile and Harpoon anti-ship missiles. The Mk 13 missile launcher was removed after the SM-1MR was phased out of U.S. service, but remains installed on OHP in foreign navies, leaving the OHP with a very limited air defense capability and no strike capability. The [128]OHP class frigates have facilities for two SH-60 helicopters.[129]

B.   LITTORAL COMBAT SHIP (LCS)

The LCS program is one of the most unique concepts ever attempted by the Navy. The capabilities of the LCS are supposed to revolutionize how the Navy operates, especially in the littoral region. By incorporating modular design features into a common hull type, each LCS should be able to undertake a variety of missions for a reduced cost. Each LCS hull is built with only a minimum of installed capabilities and is to be operated by a minimum number of personnel. The actual capabilities of the ship will come from the installed mission modules. The LCS hull has space set aside for the installation of one of three different mission modules, which will allow the LCS to conduct that specific mission. The modularity of the LCS hull is designed to allow the mission modules to be changed out rapidly while in port as the need for additional capabilities in a region evolve. In the early 1990s, the Navy realized that the ending of the Cold War and the changing international security environment required that the Navy begin to evolve as well.

The genesis of the LCS can be traced to the end of the Cold War and the shift in Navy strategy away from preparing to fight a monolithic, continental enemy to being an expeditionary force designed to handle multiple regional conflicts. Both the 1992

---

[126] Ibid.

[127] Ibid.

[128] Ibid.

[129] Ibid.

31

...From the Sea and the 1994 *Forward...From the Sea* white papers discuss the need of the Navy to increasingly operate in the littoral regions that were not traditionally part of blue water fleet operations.[130] In the mid-1990s, the Navy conducted a series of wargames to help to identify the sorts of technologies and vessels that would be useful in littoral combat. Utilizing state of the art modeling and simulation technology, the Navy was able to evaluate a number of developmental platforms and systems. Among the unmanned systems evaluated: were unmanned aerial vehicles (UAV), unmanned underwater vehicles (UUV), unmanned surface vehicles (USV), airborne surface warfare and mine countermeasures systems, and hypothetical platforms and weapons systems. Played against the backdrop of the Straits of Hormuz, these wargames identified a number of problems with the current fleet that greatly affected their ability to operate in the littoral region. Specifically, the results of the wargames demonstrated that the fleet, while capable of handling the task of littoral combat, was not the ideal. What should have been a simple and quick operation, ended up lasting a number of simulated weeks. Large surface combatants ended up with heavy damage from the expected sources (shore-based aircraft, submarines, and shore-based anti-ship missile batteries), and from unexpected sources (mines and gunboats). The results of these wargames led to the realization that the Navy needed a ship capable of operating in the littoral regions. The Navy needed a smaller class of ship to operate effectively in the littoral region. These ships were imagined to be expendable, more than the larger, traditional warships. Later war gaming found that the LCS (as initially designed) was also ideal for maritime interdiction, intelligence collection, the escort of larger ships through the littoral region, and support of special forces operations.[131] The Navy's continuing evolution towards operating in the littoral regions resulted in the development of the *Streetfighter* concept of the late 1990s. In 1998, Vice Admiral Arthur Cebrowski developed four themes that he

---

[130] Sean O'Keefe, Frank B. Kelso II, and C.E. Mundy, Jr, , *...From the Sea,* (Washington, DC: Department of Defense, September 1992). John H. Dalton, J.M. Boorda, and C.E. Mundy, Jr, *Forward...From the Sea* (Washington, DC: Department of Defense, 1994).

[131] Robert Carney Powers, "Birth of the Littoral Combat Ship," *Proceedings Magazine,* September 2012, accessed March 1, 2013, http://www.usni.org/magazines/proceedings/2012-09-0/birth-littoral-combat-ship.

believed to be essential to the future of maritime power in the United States.[132] Vice Admiral Cebrowski advocated that the Navy develop to become a network-centric force with distributed sensors and weapons systems; that the Navy needed to be able to collect, interpret, and evaluate sensor information faster than the enemy; that the Navy needed to be able overcome coastal defenses to enable air and ground forces to conduct operations in enemy territory; and that the Navy needed to increase the size of its fleet in order to ensure success in both littoral combat and peacetime missions.[133] These four themes led to the development of the *Streetfighter*.

The *Streetfighter* concept divided the fleet up into two groups, the Economy A forces and Economy B forces.[134] The Economy A force was composed of the traditional fleet. These ships would continue to provide the power projection and strike capabilities to the Navy. The Economy B force, or the *Streetfighter* ships, would be new class of ships with a displacement of less than 1000 tons that were designed to employ networked capabilities and maneuver to fight in the littoral regions. Most importantly, these ships would have significant organic offensive capability and some degree of modularity that would allow them to operate independently or at the squadron or fleet levels.[135] The ships in the Economy B force were supposed to be affordable and expendable. The distributed and networked nature of this force meant that the loss of one ship would not significantly reduce the overall combat effectiveness of the force, like the loss of a single ship would from the Economy A forces.[136]

In late July 2000, the Chief of Naval Operations, Admiral Vern Clark, ordered a study be conducted on the feasibility of the *Streetfighter* concept. Following soon afterwards, the 2001 Quadrennial Defense Review mandated a change in the future fleet

---

[132] A. K. Cebrowski, and Wayne P. Hughes, Jr., "Rebalancing the Fleet," *Proceedings Magazine*, November 1999, accessed March 1, 2013, http://www.usni.org/magazines/proceedings/1999-11/rebalancing-fleet.

[133] Ibid.

[134] Ibid.

[135] Ibid.

[136] Duncan Long and Stuart Johnson, *The Littoral Combat Ship: From Concept to Program* (Washington, DC: Center for Technology and National Security Policy, March 2007, 4.

of the Navy. What was originally supposed to be a single, advanced combatant (the DD-21 program) was broken up into three ships (the DD(X), CG(X), and LCS).[137] On 1 November 2001, the LCS program was officially stood up with the creation of the LCS Program Office. The LCS program office decided that the LCS would be a modular design and would have three primary missions. These three missions are antisubmarine warfare (ASW), mine countermeasures (MCM), and surface warfare (SUW) in the littorals. Secondary to the three primary missions, the LCS would be able to conduct maritime engagement and partnership, maritime intercept, surveillance and intelligence gathering, the support of special forces, and homeland defense missions. As of December 2012, the Navy intends to procure 55 LCS and 64 mission modules (16 ASW, 24 MCM, 24 SUW).[138] The Navy intended that each LCS would take two years to build at a cost of $260 million, but now it is estimated that each LCS will take three years to build at a cost of almost $700 million.[139]

In 2004, the Navy awarded contracts to both Lockheed Martin and General Dynamics to design two different versions of the LCS. Each version of the LCS is being constructed to a radically different design and with radically different sensors and combat systems. The Lockheed Martin variant of the LCS is being constructed at Marinette Marine Shipyard in Marinette, Wisconsin. The General Dynamics version of the LCS is being constructed at the Austral USA shipyard in Mobile, Alabama.

---

[137] Long and Johnson, *The Littoral Combat Ship*, 8.

[138] CRS, *Navy Littoral Combat Ship (LCS) Program*, 1-2.

[139] CBO, *Options for Combining the Navy's and the Coast Guard's Small Combatant Programs*, 9; U.S. Naval Institute, "Navy Defends Monday's LCS Contract Award," accessed March 5, 2013, http://news.usni.org/2013/03/05/navy-defends-mondays-lcs-contract-award.

1.   *Freedom* class

Figure 2.   USS *Freedom* (LCS-1) (From IHS Jane's, 2012)

The *Freedom* (LCS-1) class of Littoral Combat Ship has a length of 378.3 feet, a beam of 57.4 feet, a draft of 13.5 feet, and a full load displacement of 3354 tons.[140] Two Rolls Royce MT-30 gas turbine engines and two Fairbanks Morse Colt-Pielstick 16PA6B diesel engines in a Combined Diesel and Gas (CODAG) arrangement power the *Freedom* class ships. The CODAG arrangement allows the ship to operate on either the gas turbine or the diesel engines, depending on how much power is needed. These four engines power four Rolls Royce Kamewa 153SII waterjets and give the *Freedom* class a maximum speed of 40 knots and a maximum range of 3500 nautical miles at 14 knots.[141] The *Freedom* class ships have a crew of 60 personnel with space for an additional 15 as part of the aviation detachment and 25 as part of the mission module detachment.[142]

---

[140] "Freedom Class Littoral Combat Ship Flight 0," *IHS Jane's*, July 25, 2012.

[141] Ibid.

[142] Ibid.

The *Freedom* class ships are equipped with an EADS TRS-3D air and surface search radar, a Sperry Bridgemaster navigation radar, and a FABA DORNA fire control radar.[143] The *Freedom* class has no installed sonar.[144]

The *Freedom* class ships are armed with a BAE Systems 57 millimeter/70 caliber gun system, four 12.7-millimeter machine guns, and a Raytheon Rolling Airframe Missile RIM-116 Mk 99 surface-to-air missile (SAM) launcher.[145] Additional weapons capabilities can be added with the addition of mission modules. The *Freedom* class ships have a hangar large enough for either two MH-60 R/S helicopters or a single MH-60 R/S helicopter and three vertical takeoff UAV.[146]

2. *Independence* class

Figure 3.   USS *Independence* (LCS-2) (From IHS Jane's, 2012)

---

[143] Ibid.

[144] Ibid.

[145] Ibid.

[146] Ibid.

The *Independence* (LCS-2) class ships have a length of 417 feet, a beam of 103 feet, a draft of 14.8 feet, and a full load displacement of 2841 tons.[147] The *Freedom* class ships are powered by two General Electric LM2500 gas turbine engines and two MTU 20V 8000 diesel engines arranged as CODAG which power four Wärtsilä waterjets and a single steerable thruster unit. The *Independence* class has a maximum speed of 40 knots and a maximum range of 3500 nautical miles at 14 knots.[148] The LCS-2 class ships have a crew of 60 personnel with space for an additional 15 personnel as part of the air detachment and 25 personnel as part of the mission module detachment.[149]

The *Independence* class ships are equipped with an Ericson Sea Giraffe air and surface search radar, a Sperry Bridgemaster navigation radar, and a Seastar Safire III fire control radar.[150] The *Independence* class littoral combat ships have no installed sonar.[151]

The *Independence* class ships have a BAE Systems 57 millimeter/70 caliber gun system, four 12.7-millimeter machine guns, a Raytheon RAM RIM-116 Mk 99 surface-to-air missile launcher organic to the ship.[152] Additional weapons capabilities can be added with the addition of mission modules. The *Independence* class ships have hangar space for a MH-60 R/S helicopter and three vertical takeoff UAVs.[153]

3. Modules

The LCS is designed to be modular. Essential to the modular concept of the LCS are the modules that provide the enhanced capabilities in the form of three unique mission packages (MP). The three modules are the SUW module, the ASW module, and the MCM module.[154] Each of these mission modules is designed to fit within the

---

[147] "Independence Class Littoral Combat Ship Flight 0," *IHS Jane's*, July 25, 2012.

[148] Ibid.

[149] Ibid.

[150] Ibid.

[151] Ibid.

[152] Ibid.

[153] Ibid.

[154] "Freedom Class Littoral Combat Ship Flight 0," *IHS Jane's*, July 25, 2012; "Independence Class Littoral Combat Ship Flight 0," *IHS Jane's*, July 25, 2012.

standard 10 and 20 foot containers to ease the transport and storage of the modules.[155]
The LCS MP concept is a three-tiered approach to capabilities and equipment. The first
layer is the mission system (MS). The MS is composed of the various vehicles, weapons,
and additional sensors that give the ships the additional capabilities. The next level, the
mission modules (MM), consists of the MS with the addition of the various pieces of
support equipment needed to operate the MS on the LCS. The final layer, the MP,
consists of the MM, the assigned personnel, and the aviation assets.[156]

a.   SUW Module

The SUW MP is designed to give the LCS the ability to combat the small
boat threat. The first component of the SUW MP is the surface-to-surface MM, which
consists of the surface-to-surface missile MS. The surface-to-surface MS consists of the
missiles, launchers, and the control systems associated with the targeting and launch of
the missiles.[157] The intended mission, a joint Army-Navy program called the Non-Line
of Sight Launch System (NLOS-LS), was canceled and replaced by the AGM-176 Griffin
missile already in use with the Army and Air Force.[158] The second component, the Gun
MM, consists of two Mk 44 30-millimeter gun systems and the associated ammunition
and storage.[159] The third MM is Maritime Security MM. The Maritime Security MM
consists of two 11-meter rigid hulled inflatable boats, the boarding teams, all their
required gear, and assorted habitation modules.[160] The final MM adds Hellfire missiles
and 12.7- and 7.62-millimeter machine guns to the helicopter.[161]

---

[155] "Littoral Combat Ships – Mission Modules," U.S. Navy, accessed February 10, 2013,
http://www.navy.mil/navydata/fact_display.asp?cid=2100&tid=406&ct=2.

[156] Ibid.

[157] "Littoral Combat Ships - Surface Warfare (SUW) Mission Package," U.S. Navy, accessed
February 10, 2013, http://www.navy.mil/navydata/fact_display.asp?cid=2100&tid=437&ct=2.

[158] Ibid.

[159] Ibid.

[160] "Freedom class littoral combat ship flight 0," *IHS Jane's*, July 25, 2012; "Independence class
Littoral combat ship flight 0," *IHS Jane's*, July 25, 2012; "Littoral Combat Ships - Surface Warfare (SUW)
Mission Package," U.S. Navy, accessed February 10, 2013,
http://www.navy.mil/navydata/fact_display.asp?cid=2100&tid=437&ct=2.

[161] "Freedom class littoral combat ship flight 0," *IHS Jane's*, July 25, 2012; "Independence class
Littoral combat ship flight 0," *IHS Jane's*, July 25, 2012; "Littoral Combat Ships - Surface Warfare (SUW)
Mission Package," U.S. Navy, accessed February 10, 2013,
http://www.navy.mil/navydata/fact_display.asp?cid=2100&tid=437&ct=2.

b.   ASW Module

The current LCS ASW MP is only partially developed and relies heavily on deployable manned and unmanned systems. It was determined to be inadequate for the ASW mission and a second generation MP has been proposed.[162] The second generation ASW MP consists of the ASW escort module, the torpedo defense module, the aviation module, and the mission management center.[163] The ASW escort MM will consist of a variable depth sonar (VDS), a multi-function towed array (MFTA), the launching and recovery equipment for both sonar systems, and the signal processing systems.[164] The torpedo defense MM will consist of the MFTA with acoustic intercept capabilities to detect incoming torpedoes and the lightweight towed torpedo countermeasure system.[165] The Aviation MM will consist of the MH-60R helicopter with the airborne low frequency sonar system and two UAVs.[166] The second generation ASW MP is expected to enter service in 2016.[167]

c.   MCM Module

The LCS MCM MP is still under development but is designed around multiple manned and unmanned systems that would allow the LCS to find and neutralize mines while remaining outside the minefield.[168] The MP currently consists of advanced airborne detection and neutralization equipment. The MH-60S helicopter will tow the AQS-20A minehunting sonar, the AN/WLD-1 remote multi-mission vehicle, or the Airborne Laser Mine Detection System (ALMDS). Mines will be destroyed using the helicopter deployed Rapid Airborne Mine Clearance System or the Airborne Mine

---

[162] "Littoral Combat Ships - Surface Warfare (ASW) Mission Package," U.S. Navy, accessed February 10, 2013, http://www.navy.mil/navydata/fact_display.asp?cid=2100&tid=412&ct=2.

[163] Ibid.

[164] Ibid.

[165] Ibid.

[166] Ibid.

[167] Ibid.

[168] "Littoral Combat Ships - Mine Countermeasures (MCM) Mission Package," U.S. Navy, accessed February 10, 2013, http://www.navy.mil/navydata/fact_display.asp?cid=2100&tid=437&ct=2.

Neutralization System. For mine sweeping operations, the MH-60S is equipped with the Organic Airborne and Surface Influence Sweep.[169]

C. CONCLUSION

The primary HD platform of the U.S. Navy, the *OHP* frigate, is being decommissioned due to age and is supposed to be replaced by the *LCS*. The LCS is designed to provide the U.S. Navy with the ability to conduct a variety of HD mission and traditional military missions, including the ability to conduct maritime security operations with the SUW module, conduct shallow water ASW with the ASW module, and mine clearance operations with the MCM module. The questions are whether it is the right ship for the mission and whether it can be procured efficiently within the current budget-constrained environment. The next chapter examines these issues.

---

[169] "Freedom Class Littoral Combat Ship Flight 0," *IHS Jane's*, July 25, 2012; "Independence Class Littoral Combat Ship Flight 0," *IHS Jane's*, July 25, 2012.

V. CRITIQUES OF CURRENT PLANS

This chapter summarizes the various critiques of U.S. Navy plans for the future of the fleet, both in terms of fleet composition and the LCS. The fleet has remained almost unchanged in design since the Second World War. That fleet was designed to conduct major fleet operations against a similarly arranged combatant and to conduct amphibious operations. But the evolving modern security environment has changed the requirements for the fleet. This chapter then examines the LCS program and the many challenges and problems associated with its development and operations.

A. FLEET COMPOSITION

Since the end of the Cold War, there have been a number of studies conducted concerning the ideal composition of the fleet. The composition of the U.S. fleet has remained relatively unchanged since the Second World War. The U.S. fleet has been designed to project power, provide deterrence, and control the seas through the use of aircraft carriers, nuclear submarines, and amphibious operations. The current fleet is capable of handling the types of missions that are associated with HD – maritime engagement, counter-narcotics, counter-piracy, and maritime security. But the design is inefficient for the task. The fleet is built around billion dollar air defense and anti-submarine platforms that are being required to work at the low end of the spectrum of operations, rather than in their primary warfare area.

In 2004, Congress ordered that the Navy conduct a study as to the future of the Navy's fleet. In 2005, the results of three independent studies were reported to Congress. Conducted by the Center for Naval Analyses (CNA), the Center for Strategic and Budgetary Analysis (CSBA), and the DoD Office of Force Transformation (OFT), each of these three potential fleet architectures propose a departure from the present fleet, though the degree to which they differ is radically different. The CNA is a federally funded research organization that works on behalf of the Navy. The CNA report is the most conservative of the three; it essentially supports the existing plan for the growth of the U.S. fleet. The CSBA report imagines a fleet slightly more radical than the CNA report. The CSBA fleet utilizes a very similar architecture to the existing fleet with only a few additional platforms to fill the gaps. Unlike the CNA and the CSBA, the OFT was part of the DoD until it was disestablished in 2006. Headed by one of the biggest proponents for radical transformation in the fleet, retired Admiral Arthur Cebrowski, the OFT report imagines a radically different fleet composition that is designed to conduct operations across the entire spectrum of conflict in the 21st Century.[170]

1. CNA Report

The most conservative model of an alternative fleet architecture, the CNA model, serves to justify the current composition of the fleet and the current plans for fleet modernization. Analyzed using the preexisting DoD models and approaches, the CNA report proposes a fleet with a design very similar to the Navy fleet at the time. The fleet is still centered on the traditional CSG and ESG units with the addition of the LCS to fill the low-end combatant gap.[171] The only revolutionary concept with this study is that it serves to justify either fleet expansion or fleet reduction.[172]

2. CSBA Report

The CSBA report falls between the CNA report and the OFA report. It is more conservative than the first but also suggests some modification of the structure of the current fleet, as does the OFT report. The majority of the fleet suggested in this report is unchanged from what presently exists. Unlike the OFT report's complete redesign of the fleet, the CSBA report only suggests the production of multiple classes of aircraft carriers. The fleet would be designed around both large and medium-deck aircraft carriers, amphibious ships, cruisers, destroyers, and the LCS.[173] The combination of both large and medium-sized aircraft carriers allows the fleet to provide more global coverage with similar levels of manning.

---

[170] CRS, *Navy Force Structures, 10.*

[171] Ibid., 2

[172] Ibid.

[173] Ibid., 6.

3.   OFT Report

The OFT report recommends the most radical departure from the existing fleet. This report recommends the creation of eight new classes of ships and then reorganizes the fleet around them. First of all, this report recommends the building of two different types of aircraft carriers. One aircraft carrier would displace about half as much as a current CVN and the other would displace roughly equivalent to an eighth of a current CVN. In addition to both types of aircraft carriers, the report imagines a large, amphibious warship capable of both operating aircraft and launching amphibious assaults. This report also suggested the construction of a number of different types of combatants, a large missile ship, a 1000-ton surface shop, and a 100-ton surface ship. The missile ship would be a large surface combatant (approximately the same size as the suggested amphibious ship), armed with 360 VLS tubes, and be able to operate as a support ship for the smaller combatants. The small combatants would have a combination of both organic and modular capabilities, allowing them to be tailored for specific operations as needed. Finally, the OFT fleet could include support ships for the small combatants and non-nuclear submarines to support the traditional national defense mission and HD.[174]

The strength of the fleet designed in the OFT report is in numbers and advanced capabilities. By shrinking the size and complexity of the ships that make up the fleet, the same cost and manning can be spread out over more ships. Using a similar CSG and ESG arrangement as the fleet currently uses, the OFT report provides three alternative fleets, all of which at least double the current fleet numbers.[175] In order to achieve the sorts of capabilities with the more ships, the OFT report advocates smaller ships with improved payloads, network-centric warfare capabilities, and modularity.[176]

---

[174] Ibid., 3–4.

[175] Ibid., 5.

[176] Stuart E. Johnson and Arthur K. Cebrowski, *Alternative Fleet Architecture Design* (Washington, DC: National Defense University, 2005), 2–3.

B.   LCS

Since its inception, the LCS program has faced much criticism. Initially, the program faced stiff opposition for its departure from traditional ship design and as the program developed with two different hulls built, the program's problems became more than just conceptual. Critics of the program cite the extensive cost of the program, the apparent lack of survivability of the platforms, manning and problems with the modules as reasons to reevaluate the Navy's plan.

1.   Cost

The most serious problem associated with the LCS program is the cost of the project. When the program was first imagined, the cost of each LCS was estimated at $220 million.[177] But as time progressed and the programs developed, the cost of each LCS steadily expanded. Between 2005 and 2007, the cost estimate for the LCS-1 grew from $215.5 million in 2005 to $274.5 million in 2007. In that same amount of time, the cost of LCS-2 expanded from $213.7 million to $278.1 million. In both cases, the cost of each version of the LCS grew almost 30 percent in a two-year period. According to the Navy, the growth during this period was a result that the initial cost estimates of the LCS did not include many of the traditional costs associated with a Navy shipbuilding program, such as program management costs, inflation, and project growth.[178] By 2008, the cost of the LCS-1 variant had ballooned to an estimated $370 million and the estimated cost of both LCS programs had expanded to somewhere near $1.075 billion. In 2009, the program costs continued to rise. LCS-1 was estimated to cost $531 million and LCS-2 was estimated at $507 million. The FY2011 Budget continued to show the expansion of the LCS program. By 2011, the costs of the LCS-1 had somewhat steadied out at $537 million, but the cost of LCS-2 had ballooned to $575 million. By 2012, the cost of each LCS had steadied at $537 million for LCS-1 and $653 million for LCS-2, not including the final delivery costs associated with each ship. Both cost estimates do not include the expected final outfitting, post-delivery, and the Final System Design Mission

---

[177] CRS, *Navy Littoral Combat Ship*, 8.

[178] Ibid., 54.

44

Systems and Ship Integration Team costs for each vessel, which add an additional $150 million to the final cost of each ship, raising the total cost of each ship to $670.4 million for the LCS-1 and $808.8 million for LCS-2.[179] In October 2012, Rear Admiral John Kirby, the U.S. Navy's Chief of Information, responded to the many criticisms of the increasing LCS program cost. According to him, though the initial costs of the program are high, the fixed price contract of the 20 LCS program ships will eventually result in cost savings. By the time the tenth LCS is under construction, the average cost of the LCS should be under the $400 million price cap set by Congress.[180] Even though the cost of each LCS is supposed to drop as more of them are built, it is unlikely that the LCS program will ever represent the sort of cost savings imaged.

Many have tried to justify the near tripling of the cost of an LCS over a seven-year period. One possibility is that the initial estimates for both versions of the LCS were intentionally and unreasonably low in order to ensure that the Navy and the DoD commit to the program before the true costs of the program became known. But there is no evidence to support this claim.[181] Another possibility for the increase in the cost is that the application of the Naval Vessel Rules (NVR) to the LCS program resulted in significant delays and redesigns which caused the cost to increase. The NVR are a series of rules and regulations put in place by the American Bureau of Shipping and the Naval Sea Systems Command that govern the stability, structural design, propulsion plant, electrical systems, navigation systems, communication systems, and habitability of a naval ship. The Navy argues that being required to meet NVR requirements drove up the price of the LCS program and because the NVR was issued while both versions of the LCS were under construction, the Navy and the builders of the LCS were forced to constantly adjust the designs, which drove up prices.[182] Finally, the Navy also attributes some of the price increases to poor shipyard performance and the increased cost of

---

[179] Ibid., 55–57.

[180] "LCS: Let's Talk Facts," Navy Live, accessed March 17, 2013, http://navylive.dodlive.mil/2012/10/10/lcs-lets-talk-facts/.

[181] Ibid.,

[182] Ibid.,

building materials during construction.[183] But based on the studies conducted concerning the cost growth of warships, price growth due to increased building materials and shipyard costs is unlikely. The most likely reason for the incredible growth of the price of an LCS is some combination of all three factors. In the end, the Navy ended up with a ship capable of conducting low-end operations but built for the price of a modern multimission frigate.

2.   Vulnerability

One of the biggest criticisms of the LCS is that the ships are not expected to be survivable. In 1988, the U.S. Navy published OPNAVISNT 9070.1, *Survivability Policy for Surface Ships of the U.S. Navy*. This document assigned three different levels of survivability to ships with respect to how much damage in battle ships built to those standards would be able withstand. The first of these levels, Level I, provided the least amount of protection to both ship and crew. The only combatants that were designed to this level of survivability were the patrol craft and minesweepers.[184]

> Level I represents the least severe environment anticipated and excludes the need for enhanced survivability for designated ship classes to sustain operations in the immediate area of an engaged Battle Group or in the general war-at-sea region. In this category, the minimum design capability required shall, in addition to the inherent sea keeping mission, provide for EMP and shock hardening, individual protection for CBR, including decontamination stations, the DC/FF capability to control and recover from conflagrations and include the ability to operate in a high latitude environment.[185]

The second of these levels, Level II, provided more protection to ships designed to operate in conjunction with a CSG or ESG. Ships designed to this level were supposed to be able to take some weapons damage and continue combat operations for a time. Most of the ships in the Navy are currently constructed to this level. Specifically, frigates, amphibious ships and logistic ships are built to this level.[186]

---

[183] Ibid., 57–58.

[184] Chief of Naval Operations (CNO), 9070.1 *Survivability Policy for Surface Ships of the U.S. Navy* (Washington, D.C: Department of the Navy, September 23, 1988), 10.

[185] Ibid., 9.

[186] Ibid., 10.

Level II represents an increase of severity to include the ability for sustained operations when in support of a Battle Group and in the general war-at-sea area. This level shall provide the ability for sustained combat operations following weapons impact. Capabilities shall include the requirements of Level I plus primary and support system redundancy, collective protection system, improved structural integrity and subdivision, fragmentation protection, signature reduction, conventional and nuclear blast protection and nuclear hardening.[187]

The third and final level of survivability, Level III, provided the greatest protection to the ship and crew and allowed ships to be hit by multiple anti-ship missiles or torpedoes and continue operations. The only ships in the fleet that were designed to this level were the aircraft carriers, cruisers, and destroyers.[188] "Level III, the most severe environment projected for combatant Battle Groups, shall include the requirements of Level II plus the ability to deal with the broad degrading effects of damage from anti-ship cruise missiles (ASCM), torpedoes and mines."[189]

In late 2012, the Navy issued a new version of this instruction, 9070.1A. This instruction got rid of the traditional levels of survivability and replaced it with a more pragmatic approach. Survivability would no longer be broken down into distinct categories but be determined by the capabilities of the ships, rather than their characteristics and construction. According to the most recent instruction, survivability is now based on:

> This basic premise has not changed although survivability is now considered in terms of capabilities vice characteristics. The previous version established a minimum baseline of survivability. This revision recognizes the changing nature of naval ship design and system threats and eliminates the prescriptive survivability characteristics while establishing the new requirement to derive a minimum survivability baseline that is based on the programs' ICD and defined concept of operations (CONOPS). Survivability shall be addressed on all new surface ship, combat systems and equipment designs, overhauls, conversions, and

---

[187] Ibid., 9.

[188] Ibid., 10.

[189] Ibid., 9.

47

modernizations in order that the design is provided a balance of survivability performance, risk, and cost within program objectives.[190]

Initially, the LCS was to be built to what would have been described as Level I. The LCS was designed to survive in seas up to 30 feet, have installed firefighting systems, be hardened against electromagnetic pulses, and be protected against chemical, biological, and radiological attack. But the LCS was not designed to continue operations after taking combat damage.[191] Because improving the structural survivability of the LCS to Level II would be too expensive, the Navy decided that it was going to create a new level of survivability called Level I+.[192] Level 1+ places the LCS above a minesweeper but less than an *OHP* frigate in terms of survivability. Level 1+ protections include all the same protections that a Level 1 ship has, but with increased shock mounting for mechanical and damage control systems and increased armor around selected spaces.[193]

According to the Navy, the reduced survivability of the LCS is made up for in the ability of the LCS to travel at much higher speeds compared to normal ships. With expected top speeds above 40 knots, the LCS should be able to run away from any warships that could pose a danger. But this speed comes with a significant cost. Not only do the weight restrictions severely limit the LCS, but the ship's gun is less effective at high speeds, the ship's range is reduced dramatically, the sonar and minesweeping gear become ineffective, and the ship cannot launch or recover the small boats or the helicopter. Most important, the spread of anti-ship missiles around the world negates the added value of a ship capable of doing over 40 knots. With the enemy firing anti-ship missiles capable of moving at around 600 knots, the ability of the LCS to travel at 40 knots becomes moot.[194]

---

[190] Chief of Naval Operations, 9070.1A *Survivability Policy and Standards for Surface Ships and Craft of the U.S. Navy,* (Washington, DC: Department of the Navy, September 13, 2012), 4.

[191] GAO, *Navy's Ability to Overcome Challenges Facing the Littoral Combat Ship Will Determine Eventual Capabilities,* 4–5.

[192] "Navy Responds to Pentagon LCS Survivability Claims," U.S. Naval Institute News, accessed March 16, 2013, http://news.usni.org/2013/01/17/navy-responds-pentagon-lcs-survivability-claims.

[193] CRS, *Navy Littoral Combat Ship,* 24.

[194] Vego, "No Need for High Speed."

3. Manning

Another concern with the LCS program is that the reduced manning concept of the LCS has a negative impact on readiness and safety. The LCS was designed to be operated by a minimum number of crew in order to cut down on manning costs. The initial estimates for the core crew of a LCS were 40 personnel, with an additional 40 coming as part of the aviation detachment and MM detachment, which brought the total manning of an LCS up to 80. But even with advanced automation and crew reduction measures being used throughout the ship and a the majority of the ships logistical needs being managed from units ashore, the workload on the crew was enormous and fatigue would greatly reduce the effectiveness of the LCS.[195]

In July 2012, the Navy decided to increase the core crew of the LCS by 20 people, bringing the total crew of the ship up to 100. In addition, the LCS will deploy with a rotational crew concept, similar to what is used on the Fleet Ballistic Missile Submarines. The Navy intends to man each LCS using a three crew for every two LCS model. The ships will remain forward deployed for 16 months at a time and the individual crews will deploy out to the ships on four month cycles. The theory behind this plan is that it will allow the LCS to remain deploy for longer periods of time than traditional manning models allow.[196]

But even with the increased crew size and decreased deployment time, fatigue will still set in quicker on the LCS than on a traditional ship and reduce the safety and readiness of the personnel on the ship. The reduced manning leads to more time spent on watch both in port and underway. This translates into less time available to perform maintenance and upkeep on the ships. Combined with the legal prohibition against foreign workers performing certain types of essential maintenance on U.S. warships, the material condition of the LCS will continuously decline.[197]

---

[195] CRS, *Navy Littoral Combat Ship*, 5.

[196] Ibid.

[197] Christopher P. Cavas, "Maintenance Hurdles Mount for New USN Ship," DefenseNews, accessed February 23, 2013, http://www.defensenews.com/article/20120723/DEFREG02/307230006/Maintenance-Hurdles-Mount-New-USN-Ship?odyssey=tab%7Ctopnews%7Ctext%7CFRONTPAGE.

4.   Modules

Without the correct module installed, the LCS has only a limited offensive capability. In an ideal situation, an LCS would deploy with one module installed and operate in that role until a new situation developed that would require the LCS to rush back to port, switch out the old module and replace it with the correct one in 24 hours and proceed on its new mission with a new set of abilities. But in reality this concept, seems to not work as designed and only offers limited benefits. Countries, such as Denmark, have used modular weapon systems and capabilities on their ships successfully, but never to such an extent that the ship must have no modules to perform its several tasks.

During the initial war-gaming for the LCS, a number of issues were identified concerning the modular design. One of the biggest problems is that the support infrastructure needed to change out the modules is often not available in the types of austere ports out of which the LCS is expected to operate. Ports in these regions are often small and not equipped to support a U.S. Navy presence in them. Additionally, in these same war games, the opposing forces were able to severely hamper the usefulness of the LCS by targeting the facilities needed to change out the modules. Without the ability to switch modules, the effectiveness of the LCS in combat operations was greatly reduced.[198] Another problem exposed during the games was that the time needed to switch out the modules began limiting the usefulness of the LCS. The original concept was based on a 24-hour change out cycle. But as the modules became more complex and the concept became more developed, the time needed to change a module grew. An optimistic current estimate for the time needed is 96 hours but in actuality it is expected to take even longer, especially when operating overseas from an austere port. But with very few complete modules, the actual time needed to change out a module in a foreign port is only an estimate.[199]

There are other problems pending. The two main components of the MCM module do not work as previously thought. A 2011 report by the DoD Operational Test

---

[198] Powers, "Birth of the Littoral Combat Ship."

[199] Christopher Cavas, "LCS: Quick Swap Concept Dead," DefenseNews, accessed March 1, 2013, http://www.defensenews.com/article/20120714/DEFREG02/307140001/LCS-Quick-Swap-Concept-Dead.

and Evaluation Office identified some of them. The report found that both the AN/AQS-20A Sonar Mine Detecting Set and the ALMDS are "deficient" in their primary role.[200] The ALMDS is unable to detect mines while operating at its maximum depth and is unable to classify mines while operating at surface depths.[201] The SUW module has experienced similar problems to the MCM module. Initially, the SUW was supposed to come equipped with a joint Navy and Army missile system known NLOS-LS. This missile was designed to give the LCS a missile capable of targeting enemies at a range of 25 nautical miles. When this program was canceled in 2011, the NLOS-LS was replaced with the Griffin missile.[202] Without the NLOS-LS, the LCS SUW module is limited to a 3.5 nautical miles offensive capability.[203]

---

[200] Director, Operational Test and Evaluation, "Littoral Combat Ship (LCS)," *FY2011 Annual Report,* (Washington, DC: Department of Defense, December 2011), 141.

[201] GAO, *Navy's Ability to Overcome Challenges Facing the Littoral Combat Ship Will Determine Eventual Capabilities,* 17-18.

[202] Cavas, "LCS: Quick Swap Concept Dead."

[203] GAO, *Navy's Ability to Overcome Challenges Facing the Littoral Combat Ship Will Determine Eventual Capabilities,* 19-20.

THIS PAGE INTENTIONALLY LEFT BLANK

VI. ALTERNATE SOLUTIONS

The existing composition of the U.S. fleet is well designed to handle the traditional power projection role of the national strategy and the role of the LCS is supposed to fill the low-intensity gaps that the modern fleet inefficiently handles. But both the LCS and the current fleet architecture are not the right answer for the types of homeland defense missions that the Navy finds itself operating in.

The current force structure of the U.S. Navy leaves a significant gap in the fleet. The current fleet leaves the Navy adequately prepared to handle strategic deterrent, unopposed power projection, and sea control, but too few ships for forward presence. The increasing number of nontraditional missions that the U.S. Navy finds itself engaged in require more and different ships. Most importantly, the Navy needs to ensure that these ships are able to handle the variety of modern missions that fall outside the traditional scope of naval operations, yet still can play a role in traditional fleet operations when needed. Frigate and corvette-sized ships have been the mainstay of small, modern navies around the world since the end of the Second World War. Ships of these two classes are able to provide many of the capabilities of larger ships, but at a more reasonable price and with smaller manning requirements. Additionally, frigates and corvettes are ideally suited for the HD mission. They have the long operational range and endurance needed to conduct counter-piracy operations and counter-narcotics patrols in remote waters. The weapons and sensor systems are more suited for the low to medium intensity conflict areas where maritime security and engagement missions occur. And their small size and shallow draft lets them operate close to shore and in underdeveloped ports. They are better suited to conduct training with partner-nations without overwhelming them with capabilities and technologies that are beyond the scope of what is needed.

Corvettes are generally well-suited for these roles. Corvettes displace between 500 tons and 2500 tons and are normally armed with a small- to medium-caliber gun, limited surface-to-surface missiles, and four to eight surface-to-air missiles. Corvettes tend to have decent anti-submarine warfare capabilities, especially in shallow waters.[204] Corvettes were traditionally assigned coastal patrol missions, but in modern navies, the corvette excels at protection of maritime infrastructure, counter-narcotics patrols, and counter-piracy.

Slightly larger than corvettes, frigates traditionally displace between 2500 tons and 4000 tons. Like corvettes, frigates are normally armed with small- to medium-caliber guns, surface-to-air missiles, surface-to-surface missiles, but are often afforded a more robust strike or air-defense capacity due to their larger size. Traditionally, frigates were used to provide open ocean escort to convoys and conduct anti-submarine operations. Since the end of the Cold War, frigates have proven themselves to excel in a variety of non-traditional missions, while still maintaining their ability to locate and destroy submarines. Additionally, many nations with extended maritime claims rely on the long endurance provide by frigates to conduct patrols throughout their waters in support of the counter-narcotic, counter-proliferation, counter-smuggling, and counter-immigration missions away from normal logistical support. High sprint speeds of 40 to 45 knots is not thought to be cost effective for either class of vessel.

Both corvettes and frigates provide the unique blend of low cost and low manning, with the multiple capabilities needed in the modern threat environment and in support of the homeland defense mission. The U.S. Navy is in need of a true modern frigate or corvette type ship and there are three options available: the corvette, a modular frigate, or a true patrol frigate.

A.   ALTERNATE FORCE STRUCTURE

There has been little written about the effect that force structure has on the U.S. Navy operations and how that relates to the ability of the Navy to conduct operations across the entire spectrum. In 2009, Captain Hughes suggested a radical departure from any previously existing fleet organization in his team's study entitled *The New Navy Fighting Machine*. In this study, he suggests that the U.S. Navy needs to radically

---

[204] Alex Pape, "In a class of their own: new corvettes take centre stage," *IHS Jane's*, accessed March 1, 2013, http://www.janes.com/products/janes/defence-security-report.aspx?ID=1065926963.

redesign the fleet around existing and hypothetical ship designs in order to reflect the changing international maritime security environment. Instead of the 300-ship Navy of the current fleet, the fleet reflected in this study would be over 600 ships with the majority of them being designed for combat in the littoral regions for the same cost. What would make this fleet unique is that it was designed to maintain the present levels of shipbuilding funding and manning requirements.[205] The small surface combatants in this fleet would be divided between what Hughes calls the "Forces for Theater Security and Coastal Combat Operations" and the "Surface Combatants." But for the sake of simplicity, they will be described as the Green Water Fleet and the Blue Water Fleet.

The Green Water Fleet was designed to give the U.S. Navy maximum operational flexibility in the littoral environment. To do this, the first level of the fleet was designed to provide both security and training to partner-nation navies in order to develop their capabilities. To do this, the Navy would maintain a fleet of approximately 400 inshore patrol craft.[206] These patrol craft would be used to provide maritime security and conduct counter-piracy and counter-narcotics patrols in the littoral regions and provide training to local navies. At the end of their five-year service life in the U.S. Navy, Hughes suggests giving these ships directly to the partner-nations. The next tier up from the inshore patrol craft would be the offshore patrol craft. These ships would have a similar mission to the inshore patrol boats but provide coverage farther out from shore. They would remain in U.S. service for their entire life span.[207] Finally, the Green Water Fleet would be rounded out with *Streetfighter*-like fast attack ships to provide a significant offensive capability in the littorals. In support of these three layers of ships would be a number of logistical and maintenance support ships, gunfire support ships, mine clearance ships, and light aircraft carriers, similar to the existing LHA and LHD designs.[208]

---

[205] Hughes, *The New Navy Fighting Machine*, 7.

[206] Ibid., 23–24.

[207] Ibid.

[208] Ibid.

The Blue Water Fleet would remain relatively similar to what currently exists, but would be altered to reflect the current realities of maritime combat. Hughes recommends keeping the current nuclear powered aircraft carriers, but gradually reducing their numbers to six. The reduced number of large aircraft carriers would be augmented with the construction of about ten smaller aircraft carriers for helicopters and short take off jets.[209] Strike capability in this fleet would be maintained with a number of land attack ships, which are armed with nothing but cruise missiles, with a design similar to the Arsenal ship but carrying 50 cruise missiles, instead of 500. The destroyer would continue to play the role of the air-defense ship, but the anti-surface and anti-submarine missions would be taken over by a new class of frigates.[210]

The fleet imaged in *The New Navy Fighting Machine* would be uniquely capable for conducting operations in support of HD. The ships of both the Green Water Fleet and the Blue Water Fleet would be able to conduct operations across the entire spectrum of HD missions. The patrol boats and offshore patrol ships would be ideal for the counter-piracy and counter-narcotics mission. And because the patrol boats are designed to be given to the partner-nations after five years, they are ideal to use for maritime security capacity building. The offshore patrol boats of the Green Water Fleet and the multi-mission frigates of the Blue Water Fleet would be ideal for conducting operations across the entire spectrum HD missions and should be pursued for procurement by the U.S. Navy. And because these ships cost much less and require less manning than the LCS and the *Arleigh Burke* destroyers that make up fleet, they can be procured at a greater rate and increase the number of ships in the fleet. A number of ships around the world exist that would fit the description of the offshore patrol ship or the multi-mission frigate.

B.   ALTERNATE SHIP TYPES

1.   Corvette

The smallest option for the U.S. Navy would be the construction of a class of corvettes that could be used in the offshore patrol boat role suggested in *The New Navy*

---

[209] Ibid., 49–50.

[210] Ibid.

Fighting Machine. The *Streetfighter* concept called for the construction of a class of small, high-speed vessels that would be armed with surface-to-surface missiles, anti-ship missiles, and machine guns designed to operate in the crowded and shallow littoral regions and these vessels would be similar to that concept. Vessels of this type are somewhat larger than a fast attack boat, with a displacement between 500 to 1000 tons and a crew approximately 50 people but retain the high-speed capability of the fast attack boats. These ships are able to operate independently or in squadrons of a four to eight ships each. Their small size allows for high speed and rapid maneuvering, but at the expense of endurance.

Both the Swedish and Israeli navies have found a place for corvette-sized ships in their fleets. Ideally suited for littoral combat and homeland defense, both the Swedish *Visby* class and the Israeli *Eilat* (*Sa'ar 5*) classes provide significant offensive capacity for a minimal cost. Both the *Visby* and the *Eilat* corvettes provide both the small size and stealth characteristics of the LCS. But unlike the LCS, both corvettes maintain their ability to provide a strong surface and subsurface attack and still operate freely in the littoral region. The *Eilat* (*Sa'ar 5*) is an ideal candidate for purchase by the U.S. Navy. It is designed and built by an American shipyard and equipped mostly with proven technologies that are already in the U.S. inventory, which would keep the costs down.

a.   Visby class

Figure 4.   *HMS Helsingborg* (K32) (From IHS Jane's, 2011)

The *Visby* class was first designed during the final years of the Cold War and entered the Swedish fleet in the 1990s as part of a modernization program for the Swedish Navy. Intended to fight in the littoral regions of the Swedish coast and the Baltic Sea, the *Visby* class is designed to handle a variety of missions. Built for less than $200 million, these ships are able to conduct sea control, antisubmarine warfare, mine countermeasures, mine laying, air defense, surveillance, patrol, escort, search and rescue, and civilian support operations.[211]

The *Visby* class corvettes have a length of 240 feet, a beam of 34 feet, a draft of 7.9 feet and displace approximately 630 tons.[212] The *Visby* class vessels are constructed with stealth in mind. The hull is constructed of a non-magnetic carbon fiber composite surrounding a foam core. This unique composition allows for the vessels to

---

[211] Chris Summers, "Stealth ships steam ahead," BBC News, accessed March 17, 2013, http://news.bbc.co.uk/2/hi/technology/3724219.stm; ThyssenKrupp Marine, *The VISBY Class Corvette: Defining Stealth at Sea*, 5.

[212] "Visby class (FSGH)," IHS Jane's, November 16, 2011.

have a minimum radar signature, a low infrared signature, and a low magnetic signature, while being strong enough to handle the stresses of high speed maneuvering.[213] *Visby's* are powered by a Combined Diesel or Gas (CODOG) system consisting of four TF 50A gas turbine engines and two MTU 16V 2000 N90 diesel engines. These engines can be alternately used to power the ship's two SII KaMeWa waterjets. Additionally, a HRP 200-65 Holland Roer Propeller bow thruster assists slow speed maneuvering.[214] The ships can transit at 15 knots for 2500nm using only the diesel engines or sprint up to 35 knots using the four turbines.[215] The *Visby* class corvettes have a crew of 10 officers and 43 enlisted personnel.[216]

The *Visby* class are equipped with the Ericsson Sea Giraffe AMB 3D air and surface search radar, a Terma Scanter 2001 surface search radar, and a CEROS 200 Mk 3 fire control radar.[217] For subsurface search, the *Visby* class employs a General Dynamics Hydra Suite with a bow mounted high frequency system with a Hydroscience passive towed array and VDS.[218] In addition, the *Visby* can also carry a Double-Eagle Mk III remote controlled underwater vehicle (ROV) for mine identification and detection and an expendable Atlas Elektronik Seafox ROV-E for mine destruction.

The *Visby* class is armed with a Bofors 57mm 70 SAK Mk III general-purpose gun to engage air, surface, and missile threats. The *Visby* class is equipped with four 400-millimeter torpedo tubes, capable of firing the Type 45 antisubmarine/antisurface torpedoes. Though not currently equipped, the *Visby* class ships have space allocated for the installation a surface to air missile battery.[219] In place of the mine countermeasure system, the *Visby* class can equip eight Saab RBS 15 Mk II

---

[213] *The VISBY Class Corvette: Defining Stealth at Sea*, 7-9.

[214] *The VISBY Class Corvette: Defining Stealth at Sea*, 10.

[215] Ibid; "Visby class (FSGH)," IHS Jane's, November 16, 2011.

[216] "Visby class (FSGH)," IHS Jane's, November 16, 2011.

[217] Ibid.

[218] Ibid.

[219] ThyssenKrupp Marine Systems, *The VISBY Class Corvette: Defining Stealth at Sea*, 13-14; "Visby class (FSGH)," Jane's Fighting Ships, November 16, 2011.

surface-to-surface missiles.[220] *The Visby* is capable of laying mines.[221] The *Visby* has the facilities for one Agusta Bell A109 helicopter.[222]

b. Eilat (Sa'ar 5) class

Figure 5. *INS Hanit* (503) (From IHS Jane's, 2012)

In the early 1990s, the Israeli Navy contracted the construction of a class of corvettes to replace their aging missile boats. Northrop Grumman constructed three corvettes at the Litton Ingalls shipyard in Pascagoula, Mississippi at a cost of $260 million each.[223] The *Eilat (Sa'ar 5)* class corvettes have a length of 279 feet, a beam of 39 feet, a draft of 10.5 feet, and displace 1092 tons.[224] A single LM2500 gas turbine engine and two MTU 12V TB82 diesel engines in a CODOG arrangement power the

---

[220] ThyssenKrupp Marine Systems, *The VISBY Class Corvette: Defining Stealth at Sea*, 14; "Visby class (FSGH)," Jane's Fighting Ships, November 16, 2011.

[221] ThyssenKrupp Marine Systems, *The VISBY Class Corvette: Defining Stealth at Sea*, 13-14; "Vishy class (FSGH)," Jane's Fighting Ships, November 16, 2011.

[222] ThyssenKrupp Marine Systems, *The VISBY Class Corvette: Defining Stealth at Sea*, 14.

[223] "Sons of Sa'ar? Israel's Next Generation Frigates," Defense Industry Daily, accessed March 17, 2013, http://www.defenseindustrydaily.com/an-lcs-for-israel-04065/.

[224] "Eilat (Saar 5) class (Combat Support Ships)(AGF/AKR/AH)," IHS Jane's, March 26, 2012.

ships of this class. The *Eilat* class corvettes have a maximum speed of 33 knots in the gas turbine configuration and a maximum speed of 22 knots in the diesel configuration. The ships have a range of 3500 nautical miles at a speed of 17 knots.[225] The *Eilat* corvettes are crewed by 20 officers and 74 enlisted personnel. The *Eilat* corvettes have a maximum endurance of 20 days.[226]

The *Eilat* corvettes are equipped with Elta EL/M-2218S air search radar, a Cardion SPS-55 surface search radar, and three Elta EL/M-2221 SM STGR fire control radars.[227] For subsurface search, the *Eilat* corvettes are equipped with a EDO Type 796 Mod 1 hull-mounted sonar system.[228]

Each *Eilat* corvette is equipped with either a 76 millimeter/62 caliber OTO Melara main gun, a 57 millimeter Bofors cannon, or a 20 millimeter Sea Vulcan.[229] The *Eilat* corvettes also are equipped with a number of missiles. Each vessel is armed with eight Harpoon missile canisters to attack surface vessels and two 32-cell vertical launch systems for the Israeli Industries Barak I surface-to-air missile.[230] In addition, each ship is armed with six Mk 32 324 millimeter torpedo tubes, capable of firing the Mk 46 torpedo.[231] The *Eilat* class corvettes have facilities for operating one Dauphin SA 366G or Sea Panther helicopter.[232]

---

[225] Ibid.

[226] Ibid.

[227] Ibid.

[228] Ibid.

[229] Ibid.

[230] Ibid.

[231] Ibid.

[232] Ibid.

c. *Braunschweig (K130) class*

Figure 6.   FGS *Magdeburg* (F-261) (From IHS Jane's, 2012)

Constructed by the German shipbuilding company Blohm + Voss, the *Braunschweig* (*K130*) class are part of the MEKO family of warships. Designed to be modular, MEKO type vessels allow for the vessels to be constructed cheaply with a high degree of customization for the buyer.[233]   These ships are not modular in the sense that the LCS is. They are modular in that they are constructed off of a common frame that allows the purchaser of the ship to insert the ideal sensors and weapons systems during construction for their intended missions. This class of ships is designed to provide the German Navy with a modern means of surface surveillance, antisurface warfare, humanitarian assistance, and littoral combat at a minimum cost.[234]

The *Braunschweig class* corvettes have a length of 291 feet, a beam of 43 feet, a draft of 16 feet, and displace 1870 tons.[235]   The hull and superstructure of the *Braunschweig* class are designed specifically to reduce the ship's radar cross section. The ships were also designed with multiple measures to reduce ship's infrared

---

[233] Blohm + Voss Naval, "*Corvette Class 130*," accessed February 10, 2013, https://www.blohmvoss-naval.com/en/corvette-class-130.html.

[234] Ibid.

[235] Blohm + Voss Naval, "*Corvette Class 130*," accessed February 10, 2013, https://www.blohmvoss-naval.com/en/corvette-class-130.html; "Braunschweig (K130) class (FSGHM)," *IHS Jane's*, March 2, 2012.

signature.[236] The *Braunschweig* are powered by two MTU diesel engines, capable of propelling the ships to a maximum speed of 26 knots. Bow thrusters are added for additional slow speed maneuvering. The maximum range of the *K130* corvettes is 2500 nautical miles at a speed of 15 knots.[237] The *K130* class is manned by a crew of 8 officers and 58 enlisted personnel.[238] The *K130* class corvettes are able to remain at sea for 7 days unsupported and for 21 days with the support of a tender vessel.[239]

The *K130* corvettes are equipped with the EADS TRS-3D air and surface search and fire control radar and two Raymarine Pathfinder navigation radars.[240] The *K130* are armed with a single OTO Melara 76 millimeter/62 caliber Compact gun and two Mauser 27 millimeter cannons are mounted amidships.[241] The *K130* class corvettes are also armed with four Saab RBS-15 Mk3 anti-ship missiles and two Raytheon RIM-116 Rolling Airframe Missile (RAM) batteries.[242] The *K130* class corvettes have faculties to operate one medium helicopter as well as enough additional space for two UAV.[243]

2.   Modular Frigate

The next option for the U.S. Navy is the development of a modular frigate. The capabilities of the LCS are limited to only the module that is installed on the ship. The LCS has no organic air defense capabilities and no installed sonar, which severely limits the ability of the LCS to operate in a constantly evolving battlespace. A modular frigate retains the traditional capabilities of a frigate, but can be augmented with increased anti-

---

[236] Blohm + Voss Naval, *"Corvette Class 130,"* accessed February 10, 2013, https://www.blohmvoss-naval.com/en/corvette-class-130.html.

[237] Blohm + Voss Naval, *"Corvette Class 130,"* accessed February 10, 2013, https://www.blohmvoss-naval.com/en/corvette-class-130.html; "Braunschweig (K130) class (FSGHM)," *IHS Jane's*, March 2, 2012.

[238] "Braunschweig (K130) class (FSGHM)," *IHS Jane's*, March 2, 2012.

[239] "Korvette, Braunschweig"-Klasse (K 130), accessed February 10, 2013, http://www.marine.de/portal/a/marine/!ut/p/c4/04_SB8K8xLLM9MSSzPy8xBz9CP3I5EyrpHK93MQivfL EtLTUvNI8vez8orLUkpJUvaSixNK84uSM8tTMdP2CbEdFAOmFiNM!/#par2.

[240] Blohm + Voss Naval, *"Corvette Class 130,"* accessed February 10, 2013, https://www.blohmvoss-naval.com/en/corvette-class-130.html; "Braunschweig (K130) class (FSGHM)," *IHS Jane's*, March 2, 2012.

[241] Blohm + Voss Naval, *"Corvette Class 130,"* https://www.blohmvoss-naval.com/en/corvette-class-130.html, accessed 10 February 2013; "Braunschweig (K130) class (FSGHM)," *IHS Jane's*, March 2, 2012.

[242] Blohm + Voss Naval, *"Corvette Class 130,"* accessed February 10, 2013, https://www.blohmvoss-naval.com/en/corvette-class-130.html; "Braunschweig (K130) class (FSGHM)," *IHS Jane's*, March 2, 2012.

[243] Blohm + Voss Naval, *"Corvette Class 130,"* accessed February 10, 2013, https://www.blohmvoss-naval.com/en/corvette-class-130.html.

ship, anti-aircraft, or strike capabilities as needed. The larger size of these vessels means that they are not as fast as a corvette, but also translates into a longer operational endurance, providing for a longer time on station, which can be essential when operating in remote regions.

The *Absalon* class frigates combine the best aspects of a frigate with the best aspects of a modular ship. These ships are fully functional frigates, combined with the multipurpose deck and loading ramp of an amphibious assault ship and the functionality and ease of modification of a modular ship. This combination of capabilities would make a ship similar to the *Absalon* class ideal for conduction HA/DR, engagement, and maritime security operations.

a. *Absalon class*

Figure 7. HDMS *Absalon* (L16) (From IHS Jane's, 2012)

The *Absalon* class of the Royal Dutch Navy is unique in that these ships are truly multi-mission platforms. Each ship has five *Stanflex* container positions for modular weapons systems and a Roll On/Roll off ramp, which allows access to an additional 900 square meters of multipurpose deck space. This space is capable of storing vehicles up to the size of a main battle tank, or up to 34 twenty-foot equivalent units of supplies or ammunition.[244] This deck can be converted into a command center or hospital with the installation of berthing modules.[245]

The *Absalon* class ships have a length of 450 feet, a beam of 64 feet, a draft of 21 feet, and displace 6400 tons.[246] Four MTU 8000 M70 diesel engines power the *Absalon* class support in a Combined Diesel and Diesel (CODAD) arrangement, with arranged with two engines per shaft.[247] The *Absalon* class support ships are equipped with bow thrusters for assistance in slow speed maneuvering.[248] The *Absalon* class ships have a range of 11500 nautical miles at 14 knots.[249] The *Absalon* class ships have a crew of 99 personnel but with the installation of berthing modules, can support 200 additional personnel.[250]

The *Absalon* class ships are equipped with a Thales SMART-S 3D combined air and surface search radar, a Terma Scanter 2001 surface search and navigation radar, a maximum of 4 SaabTech Ceros 200 Mk3, and a Furuno FR-2117 navigation radar.[251] For subsurface search, the *Absalon* class ships are equipped with an Atlas ASO 94 hull mounted sonar.[252] For anti-submarine missions, the *Absalom* class can be a modularized towed-array sonar system.[253]

The *Absalon* class vessels are armed with a single 5-inch/62 caliber Mk 45 Mod 4 gun and two Oerlikon Contraves 35-millimeter GDM08 guns and four 12.7-

---

[244] "Absalon class (Combat Support Ships)(AGF/AKR/AH)," *IHS Jane's*, November 19, 2012.

[245] Ibid.

[246] Ibid.

[247] Ibid.

[248] Ibid.

[249] Ibid.

[250] Ibid.

[251] Ibid.

[252] Ibid.

[253] Edward Ludquist, "Absalon-class Littoral Support Ships: 'LCS on Steroids'", accessed February 10, 2013, http://www.defensemedianetwork.com/stories/absalon-class-littoral-support-ships-lcs-on-steroids/.

millimeter machine guns.[254] In addition, the ships have five modular weapons storage areas with the capacity upgrade the *Absalon* class's anti-surface or anti-air capabilities. These five modules are able to hold a total of sixteen Harpoon Block II anti-ship missiles or 36 Evolved Sea Sparrow Missiles (RIM-162B) surface-to-air missiles.[255] All *Absalon* class ships are equipped with four 324-millimeter torpedo tubes capable of firing Eurotorp Mu 90 Impact torpedoes. The *Absalon* class has facilities for operating up to two Westland Lynx Mk 90B helicopters.[256]

3.   Patrol frigate

The final option of the Navy is the procurement of a traditional patrol frigate. Patrol frigates are designed to operate independently and without large amounts of logistic support in regions where the threat dictates air defense and antisubmarine capabilities are required, but the threat is not high enough to warrant the presence of a destroyer.   Patrol frigates are very similar to the traditional anti-air and anti-submarine frigates, but are optimized for long range patrols into remote areas without a great deal of logistical support.

A ship very similar to a patrol frigate already exists in the U.S. military. The Coast Guard's *Legend* class, also called the National Security Cutter (NSC), would be ideal for conversion into a military patrol frigate. It would not take much to provide this ship with the additional weapons and sensor systems needed for it to operate as a frigate in support of the HD mission for the Navy. The ship is already designed and built at an American shipyard to 90 percent military construction standards, which would keep the costs low.[257]

---

[254] "Absalon class (Combat Support Ships)(AGF/AKR/AH)," Jane's Fighting Ships, November 19, 2012

[255] Ibid.

[256] Ibid.

[257] U.S. Government Accountability Office, *Portfolio Management Approach Needed to Improve Major Acquisitions Outcomes*, GAO-12-918, (Washington, DC: Government Printing Office, September 2012), 34.

a.   *MEKO A-200 SAN class*

Figure 8.   SAS *Isandlwana* (F146) (From IHS Jane's, 2012)

Also known as the MEKO A-200 SAN class, the four *Valour* class frigates of the South African Navy were ordered in the late 1990s at a cost of $262 million each.[258] The *Valour* frigates have a length of 397 feet, a beam of 54 feet, a draft of 20 feet, and displace 3648 tons.[259] The *Valour* frigates are powered by a CODAG system consisting of a single LM2500 gas turbine engine and two MTU 16V 1163 TB93 diesel engines. The *Valour* class frigates also have a LiPS LJ210E waterjet located on the centerline to assist at slow speed maneuvering.[260] The *Valour* frigates have a maximum

---

[258] Leon Engelbrecht, "SA Navy Has Pick of Litter For Pending Projects," defenceWeb, accessed March 17, 2013,
http://www.defenceweb.co.za/index.php?option=com_content&task=view&id=437&Itemid=363.

[259] "Valour class (Meko A-200 SAN) (FFGHM)," Jane's Fighting Ships, March 27, 2012.

[260] Ibid; 4 Valour Class (MEKO® A200 – SAN) (FSG), accessed 10 February 2013, http://www.navy.mil.za/equipment/valour.htm.

speed of 28 knots and a maximum range of 7700 nautical miles at a speed of 15 knots.[261]
The *Valour* frigates have a crew of 20 officers and 100 enlisted.[262]

The *Valour* class frigates are equipped with a Thales MRR air and surface search radar, two Reutech RTS 6400 fire control radars, and two Racal Bridgemaster E navigation radars. For subsurface search, the *Valour* class frigates utilize a hull-mounted Thomson Marconi 4132 Kingklip sonar system.[263]

Each *Valour* class frigate is armed with a single Otobreda 76-millimeter/62 caliber compact gun system, two LIW DPG 35-millimeter guns in a twin mount, and two Reutech remote control 12.7-millimeter machine guns.[264] The *Valour* class frigates are equipped with eight MBDA Exocent MM 40 Block II anti-ship missiles and a Denel Umkhonto 32-cell vertical launch system (VLS) surface-to-air missile launcher.[265] The *Valour* class frigates have facilities for two Super Lynx helicopters.[266]

---

[261] Ibid.

[262] "Valour class (Meko A-200 SAN) (FFGHM)," *Jane's Fighting Ship,* March 27, 2012

[263] Ibid.

[264] "Valour class (Meko A-200 SAN) (FFGHM)," *Jane's Fighting Ships,* March 27, 2012; "4 Valour Class (MEKO® A200 SAN) (FSG), accessed February 10, 2013, http://www.navy.mil.za/equipment/valour.htm.

[265] "Valour class (Meko A-200 SAN) (FFGHM)," Jane's Fighting Ships, March 27, 2012

"4 Valour Class (MEKO® A200 – SAN) (FSG)", accessed February 10, 2013, http://www.navy.mil.za/equipment/valour.htm.

[266] "Valour class (Meko A-200 SAN) (FFGHM)," *Jane's Fighting Ships,* March 27, 2012

b. *Legend class*

Figure 9.   USCG *Bertholf* (WMSL-750) (From IHS Jane's, 2012)

The *Legend* class ships of the U.S. Coast Guard were designed as part of the Coast Guard's *Integrated Deepwater System* modernization program in 2002. Designed as a replacement for the aging *Hamilton* class, the NSC provide the Coast Guard with a ship able to handle all the of Coast Guard's missions as well as operate in conjunction with the U.S. Navy.[267]   The average cost of the five *Legend* class ships is $684 million dollars each.[268]

The *Legend* class cutters have a length of 418 feet, a beam of 54 feet, a draft of 21 feet, and displace 4178 tons at full load.[269]   The *Legend* class ships are powered by a CODAG system consisting of a single GE LM2500 gas turbine and two MTU20V 1163 diesel engines. For slow speed maneuvering assistance, the *Legend* class

---

[267] CBO, *Options for Combining the Navy's and the Coast Guard's Small Combatant Programs,* 10.

[268] U.S. Library of Congress, Congressional Research Service, *Coast Guard Cutter Procurement: Background and Issues for Congress*, by Ronald O'Rourke, CRS Report R42567 (Washington, DC: Office of Congressional Information and Publishing, 31 October 2012), 3-4.

[269] "Legend class (National Security Cutter)(PSOH/WMSL)," *IHS Jane's,* April 3, 2012.

ships are equipped with a bow thruster.[270] The maximum range of the *Legend* class ships is 12000 nautical miles at 9 knots and the maximum speed is 28 knots.[271] The ships of the *Legend* class are designed to be deployed for 60 to 90 days at a time for up to 230 days per year.[272] The *Legend* class ships have a crew of 14 officers and 108 enlisted personnel.[273]

The *Legend* class ships are equipped with a TRS 3D/16 surface search radar, a Hughes-Furuno SPS-73 navigation radar, and a SPQ-9B fire control radar.[274] The *Legend* class ships are armed with one Bofors 57-millimeter/70 caliber Mk 100 gun system, one General Dynamics 20-millimeter Phalanx Mk 15 system, and four 12.7-millimeter machine guns.[275] The *Legend* class ships have hangar space for one H-65 helicopter and two UAVs or for two H-65 helicopters.[276]

The designer and builder of the NSC have already designed two patrol frigate versions of the NSC. The first of them, designated the PF 4921, utilizes the same hull and propulsion system of the NSC but adds increased weapons and sensor capabilities. As designed, the PF 4921 is armed with a 76-millimeter gun, a VLS capable of launching short-range antiaircraft missiles, a Phalanx or SeaRAM close-in weapons system, eight Harpoon anti-ship missiles, and triple torpedo tubes located on the aft deck. The PF 4921 also comes with improved an improved air search compared to the NSC, a towed-array sonar, and a hull-mounted sonar system. The PF 4921 is expected to have a range of 8,000 nautical miles and an endurance of 60 days and a crew of 141. The second NSC derivate is the PF 4501. The PF 4501 is basically identical to the NSC, but

---

[270] Ibid.

[271] Ibid.

[272] Ibid.

[273] Ibid.

[274] Ibid.

[275] Ibid.

[276] Ibid.

designed for export, rather than domestic use. It keeps the same basic sensor and weapons systems as the NSC.[277]

Though the cost of the PF 4921 project is not known, the ship still is an ideal candidate for procurement on the part of the U.S. Navy; ideally the ships will cost roughly the same as the LCS. The additional weapons and sensor systems added to the ship already are proven technologies and their use, rather than technologies that are still in development, would keep the cost down and prevent the ship from being too overwhelming when being used to conduct training and operations with foreign navies.

C.   CONCLUSION

The patrol frigate and corvette are common ships among the smaller navies around the world. They are inexpensive to build and operate, require smaller crews than larger ships, and are still capable of conducting many of the missions that larger, more extensively equipped ships can. The *Eilat* corvette and PF 4921 version of the NSC would make ideal assets for the U.S. Navy, especially for the HD operations. Both ships provide the manning reductions that the LCS is supposed to provide, but still maintain the capabilities of a frigate in terms of both traditional and HD missions.

---

[277] Mrityunjoy Mazumdar, "Patrol Frigate Concepts from Huntington Ingalls Industries Gain Traction Internationally," DefenseMedianNetwork, accessed March 1, 2013, http://www.defensemedianetwork.com/stories/patrol-frigate-concepts-from-huntington-ingalls-industries-gain-traction-internationally/.

THIS PAGE INTENTIONALLY LEFT BLANK

VII. CONCLUSION

The modern U.S. Navy has never before had to contend with of missions that are now considered core competencies of the service. The Navy must efficiently contend with adversaries across the spectrum of military operations. With a number of new nations developing carrier aviation and advanced area denial and sea control weapons, it is essential that the Navy maintain a structure to retain dominance as the premier force on the planet for power projection. But, at the same time as nations such as China are rapidly modernizing their blue water navies to compete against the U.S., the need for ships capable of operating in the littoral regions in support of the variety of low to medium intensity missions that are part of homeland defense is just as demanding. The U.S. Navy needs to develop a ship that can operate at both ends of the spectrum. It must be able to support operations at the fleet level in support of power projection and sea control and be able to operate in support of the HD missions of humanitarian assistance, disaster relief and maritime security.

The HD mission requires numerous ships that are able to operate across the spectrum of operations, not just at the lowest level. The HD mission requires a ship that is capable of conducting operations in conjunction with the Coast Guard while conducting counter-narcotics patrols in the Caribbean Sea and Pacific Oceans while at the same time being able to be deployed to conduct maritime security training and engagement missions with nations around the world. And these same ships must be able to operate in conjunction with the rest of the fleet during normal fleet operations.

The Littoral Combat Ship is the Navy's attempt to build a ship capable of operating among the littoral regions of the world. The LCS is designed around a concept of modularity, allowing mission modules to be changed out while overseas, drastically altering the capabilities of the ship. But due to issues concerning the structural survivability of the ship, the ever-increasing cost of the program, reduced manning with increased demand, and the considerable difficulty to construct effective modules, the LCS program must be regarded as an experimental vessel that can be improved for the purposes for which it is intended.

Based on the research in this thesis, it is possible to make several recommendations for future policy as well as some suggestions regarding fruitful areas for additional research.

A.   RECOMMENDATIONS

- Stop construction of the LCS at the 24 ships already paid for. Operate these ships to develop the tactics and technologies needed to make the next generation of LCS a truly revolutionary ship.

- Procure a multi-mission frigate and corvette in support the fleet in the HD role like the Israeli *Eilat* class and a modern patrol frigate like the PF 4921 version of the Coast Guard's *Legend* class. Using the 55-ship LCS program as a model and the existing 10 LCS, roughly 10 PF 4921 patrol frigates and 30 *Eilat* corvettes could be purchased for the same price.

- Extend the life of the existing MCM ships and begin the procurement of a new generation of MCM ships until the technology for the LCS MCM module is more developed.

B.   FURTHER RESEARCH

This research leaves a number of questions unanswered concerning the need for a small combatant in the U.S. Navy.

- What are the procurement and operating costs of the various types of corvettes and frigates described?

- How best to integrate these small surface combatants into the existing fleet?

- How effective is the current fleet structure in relation to the variety of missions, especially the HD missions?

- Would a diesel submarine also be useful in support of the HD missions?

Though the costs should be similar to the operating costs of the frigate and minesweepers currently in operation, the U.S. Navy does not normally operate large numbers of small ships. Small combatants require additional support in terms of training and maintenance when not deployed. The answer to this question will determine if these ships do represent a cost saving measure for the U.S. Navy over the LCS program. Small combatants in the U.S. Navy traditionally only exist while their utility is needed during times of conflict. Small ships are often the first ships cut during drawdown periods because of their more limited capabilities and their tendency to not fit well within the peacetime fleet architecture. The fleet is built around the CSG and ARG structures, which have remained relatively unchanged in composition since the end of the Cold War. Both of these structures are well designed to conduct air and amphibious operations in support of sea control and power projection, but they are not optimal for operations in support of the HD mission.

THIS PAGE INTENTIONALLY LEFT BLANK

LIST OF REFERENCES

"Absalon Class (Combat Support Ships)(AGF/AKR/AH)." *IHS Jane's*. November 19, 2012.

Alkire, Brien, John Birkler, Lisa Dolan, James Dryden, Bryce Mason, Gordon T. Less, John F. Schank, and Michael Hayes. *Littoral Combat Ships: Relating Performance to Mission Package Inventories, Homeports, and Installation Sites*. Santa Monica: Rand National Defense Research Institute, 2007.

Arena, Mark, Irv Blickstein, Obaid Younossi, and Clifford Grammich. *Why Has the Cost of Navy Ships Risen?* Santa Monica: Rand National Defense Research Institute, 2006.

"Blasts Target Iraqi Oil Terminals." *BBC News*. April 25, 2004. Accessed March 1, 2013. http://news.bbc.co.uk/2/hi/middle_east/3656481.stm.

Blohm + Voss Naval. *"Corvette Class 130."* Accessed February 10, 2013. https://www.blohmvoss-naval.com/en/corvette-class-130.html.

"Braunschweig (K130) class (FSGHM)." *IHS Jane's*. March 2, 2012.

Cavas, Christopher P. "Maintenance Hurdles Mount for New USN Ship." *DefenseNews*. July 23, 2012. Accessed March 1, 2013. http://www.defensenews.com/article/20120723/DEFREG02/307230006/Maintenance-Hurdles-Mount-New-USN-Ship?odyssey=tab%7Ctopnews%7Ctext%7CFRONTPAGE.

Cavas, Christopher P. "LCS: Quick Swap Concept Dead," *DefenseNews*. July 14, 2012. Accessed February 23, 2013. http://www.defensenews.com/article/20120714/DEFREG02/307140001/LCS-Quick-Swap-Concept-Dead.

Cebrowski A. K., and Wayne P. Hughes, Jr. "Rebalancing the Fleet," *Proceedings Magazine*, November 1999. Accessed 1 March 2013. http://www.usni.org/magazines/proceedings/1999-11/rebalancing-fleet.

Central Intelligence Agency. "The World Factbook - United States." Accessed February 12, 2013. https://www.cia.gov/library/publications/the-world-factbook/geos/us.html.

Central Intelligence Agency. "The World Factbook—County Comparison: Areas." Accessed February 12, 2013. https://www.cia.gov/library/publications/the-world-factbook/rankorder/2147rank.html?countryName=United%20States&countryCode=us&regionCode=noa&rank=3#us.

Chalk, Peter. *The Maritime Dimension of International Security: Terrorism, Piracy, and Challenges for the United States*. Santa Monica: Rand National Defense Research Institute, 2008.

Congressional Budget Office. *An Analysis of the Navy's Fiscal Year 2013 Shipbuilding Plan*. Washington, DC: GPO, 2012.

Congressional Budget Office. *Options for Combining the Navy's and the Coast Guard's Small Combatant Programs*. Washington, DC: GPO, 2009.

Dalton, John H, J.M. Boorda, and C.E. Mundy, Jr,. *Forward...From the Sea*. Washington, DC: Department of Defense, 1994.

Darling, Paul T, and Justin Lawlor. "Frigates for Streetfighters." *Proceedings Magazine*, September 2011. http://www.usni.org/magazines/proceedings/2011-09/frigates-streetfighters.

Department of Defense. "About the Department of Defense (DOD)." Accessed February 7, 2013. http://www.defense.gov/about/#mission.

Department of Defense. *National Strategy for Homeland Security*. Washington, DC: GPO, October 2007.

Department of Defense. *Strategy for Homeland Defense and Civil Support*. Washington, DC: GPO, June 2005.

Deputy Chief of Naval Operations (Integration of Capabilities and Resources)(N8). *Annual Report to Congress on Long Range Plan for Construction of Naval Vessels for FY2013*. Washington, DC: Office of the Chief of Naval Operations, April 2012.

Director, Operational Test and Evaluation. "Littoral Combat Ship (LCS)." *FY2011 Annual Report*. Washington, DC: Department of Defense, December 2011.

Deputy Chief of Naval Operations (Integration of Capabilities and Resources)(N8). *Annual Report to Congress on Long-Range Plan for Construction of Naval Vessels for FY2013*. Washington, DC: GPO, 2012.

"Eilat (Saar 5) Class (Combat Support Ships)(AGF/AKR/AH)." *IHS Jane's*. 26 March 2012.

Engelbrecht, Leon. "SA Navy Has Pick of Litter for Pending Projects," defenceWeb. October 6, 2008. Accessed March 17, 2013. http://www.defenceweb.co.za/index.php?option=com_content&task=view&id=437&Itemid=363.

"Freedom Class Littoral Combat Ship Flight 0." *IHS Jane's*. July 25, 2012.

" 'Go-fast' Boats Slip by Anti-Drug Effort." *Washington Times*. April 16, 2006. Accessed February 20, 2013. http://www.washingtontimes.com/news/2006/apr/16/20060416-112558-2981r/.

Hughes, Wayne P, Jr. "The New Navy Fighting Machine: A Study of the Connections Between Contemporary Policy, Strategy, Sea Power, Naval Operations, and the Composition of the United States Fleet." NPS Study NPSOR-09-002-PR, Naval Postgraduate School, 2009.

Hughes, Wayne P, Jr. "Naval Operations: A Close Look at the Operational Level of War at Sea." *Naval War College Review 65, no. 3.* (Summer 2012): 23-47.

"Independence Class Littoral Combat Ship Flight 0." *IHS Jane's*. July 25, 2012.

Johnson, Stuart and Arthur K. Cebrowski. *Alternative Fleet Architecture Design.* Washington, DC: National Defense University, 2005.

Joint Interagency Task Force – South. *Joint Interagency Task Force Fact Sheet: Self-Propelled Semi-Submersible.*

Kline, Jeffery E. and Wayne P. Hughes, Jr. "Between Peace and the Air-Sea Battle: A War at Sea Strategy." *Naval War College Review 65, no. 4* (Autumn 2012): 35-41.

"Korvette, Braunschweig"-Klasse (K 130). Accessed February 10, 2013. http://www.marine.de/portal/a/marine/!ut/p/c4/04_SB8K8xLLM9MSSzPy8xBz9CP3I5EyrpHK93MQivfLEtLTUvNI8vez8orLUkpJUvaSixNK84uSM8tTMdP2CbEdFAOmFiNM!/#par2.

"LCS – Let's Talk Facts." *Navy Live*. October 10, 2012. Accessed March 17, 2013. http://navylive.dodlive.mil/2012/10/10/lcs-lets-talk-facts/.

"Legend class (National Security Cutter)(PSOH/WMSL)," *IHS Jane's,* April 3, 2012.

Lendon, Brad. "Two New Narco Subs Found in Columbia." CNN. September 27, 2011. Accessed February 20, 2013. http://news.blogs.cnn.com/2011/09/27/two-new-narco-subs-found-in-colombia.

Long, Duncan and Stuart Johnson. *The Littoral Combat Ship: From Concept to Program.* Washington, DC: Center for Technology and National Security Policy, March 2007.

Ludquist, Edward. "Absalon-Class Littoral Support Ships: 'LCS on Steroids.'" *Defense Media Network*. October 22, 2012. Accessed February 10, 2013. http://www.defensemedianetwork.com/stories/absalon-class-littoral-support-ships-lcs-on-steroids.

Mazumdar, Mrityunjoy. "Patrol Frigate Concepts from Huntington Ingalls Industries Gain Traction Internationally," DefenseMedianNetwork, April 24, 2012. Accessed March 1, 2013. http://www.defensemedianetwork.com/stories/patrol-frigate-concepts-from-huntington-ingalls-industries-gain-traction-internationally/.

Mendoza, Martha. "Military Wants to Expand Its Drug War in Latin America." *Navy Times*. February 3, 2013. http://www.navytimes.com/news/2013/02/SUNDAYap-us-military-expands-drug-war-in-latin-america-020213.

Murphy, Martin M. "The Unwanted Challenge." *Proceedings Magazine*, December 2008. Accessed March 1, 2013. http://www.usni.org/magazines/proceedings/2008-12/unwanted-challenge.

NATO. "Operation Ocean Shield." Allied Command Operations. Accessed March 3, 2013. http://www.aco.nato.int/page208433730.aspx.

"Oliver Hazard Perry Class (FFH)." *IHS Jane's.* April 3, 2012.

O'Keefe, Sean, Frank B. Kelso II, and C.E. Mundy, Jr. *...From the Sea.* Washington, DC: Department of Defense, September 1992.

OPNAVINST 9070.1 Survivability Policy for Surface Ships of the U.S. Navy. September 23, 1988.

OPNAVISNT 9070.1A Survivability Policy for Surface Ships and Craft of the U.S. Navy. September 13, 2012.

Pape, Alex. "In a Class of Their Own: New Corvettes Take Centre Stage," *IHS Jane's.* August 24, 2009. Accessed March 1, 2013. http://www.janes.com/products/janes/defence-security-report.aspx?ID=1065926963.

Patch, John. "The Wrong Ship at the Wrong Time." *Proceedings Magazine*, January 2011. Accessed February 21, 2013. http://www.usni.org/magazines/proceedings/2011-01/wrong-ship-wrong-time.

Popkin, Jim. "Authorities in Awe of Drug Runners' Jungle Built, Kevlar-Coated Supersubs." *Wired Magazine*. March 29, 2011. Accessed February 20, 2013. http://www.wired.com/magazine/2011/03/ff_drugsub/all/1.

Powers, Robert Carney. "Birth of the Littoral Combat Ship." *Proceedings Magazine*, September 2012. Accessed February 21, 2013. http://www.usni.org//magazines/proceedings/2012-09-0/birth-littoral-combat-ship.

Povlock, Paul. "The Coming Maritime Insurgency Century." *Proceedings Magazine*, December 2012. Accessed March 1, 2013.

http://www.usni.org/magazines/proceedings/2012-12/coming-maritime-insurgent-century.

Schlise, Chuck. "Shooting for the Middle." *Proceedings Magazine*, April 2012. Accessed February 21, 2013. http://www.usni.orgmagazines/proceedings/2012-04/shooting-middle.

South Africa Navy. "4 Valour Class (MEKO® A200 – SAN) (FSG)." May 17, 2012. http://www.navy.mil.za/equipment/valour.htm.

"Sons of Sa'ar? Israel's Next Generation Frigates." Defense Industry Daily. August 12, 2012. http://www.defenseindustrydaily.com/an-lcs-for-israel-04065/.

Stadt, Patrick H. "Industry View: Why the Navy needs a "Patrol Frigate." *DoD Buzz*. http://www.dodbuzz.com/2012/03/28/industry-view-why-the-navy-needs-a-patrol-frigate/.

Summers, Chris. "Stealth ships steam ahead." *BBC News*. June 10, 2004. Accessed March 1, 2013. http://news.bbc.co.uk/2/hi/technology/3724219.stm.

Surface Vessel Division. *The VISBY Class Corvette: Defining Stealth at Sea*. Hamburg, Germany, ThyssenKrupp Marine Systems, 2010.

United Nations Office on Drugs and Crime. "Maritime Piracy." In *The Globalization of Crime: A Transnational Organized Crime Threat Assessment*, 191-200. Vienna, Austria: United Nations, 2010.

U.S. Library of Congress. Congressional Research Service. *Coast Guard Cutter Procurement: Background and Issues for Congress,* by Ronald O'Rourke. CRS Report RL42567. Washington, DC: Office of Congressional Information and Publishing, 31 July 2012.

U.S. Library of Congress. Congressional Research Service. *Homeland Security: Navy Operations – Background and Issues for Congress*. By Ronald O'Rourke. CRS Report RS21230. Washington, DC: Office of Congressional Information and Printing, June 2, 2005.

U.S. Library of Congress. Congressional Research Service. *Navy Force Structures: Alternative Force Structures Studies of 2005 – Background for Congress*. By Ronald O'Rourke. CRS Report RL33955. Washington, DC: Office of Congressional Information and Printing, April 9, 2007.

U.S. Library of Congress. Congressional Research Service. *Navy Force Structure and Shipbuilding Plans: Background and Issues for Congress,* By Ronald O'Rourke. CRS Report RL32665. Washington, DC: Office of Congressional Information and Printing, July 26, 2012.

U.S. Library of Congress. Congressional Research Service. *Navy Littoral Combat Ship (LCS) Program: Background, Issues, and Options for Congress,* By Ronald O'Rourke. CRS Report RL33741. Washington, DC: Office of Congressional Information and Printing, December 21, 2012.

U.S. Office of the Chairman of the Joint Chiefs of Staff. *Homeland Security Joint Publication (JP) 3-26.* Washington DC: CJCS, August 2, 2005.

U.S. Office of the Chairman of the Joint Chiefs of Staff. *Civil Support Joint Publication (JP) 3-28.* Washington DC: CJCS, September 14, 2007.

U.S. Office of the Chairman of the Joint Chiefs of Staff. *Homeland Defense Joint Publication (JP) 3-27.* Washington DC: CJCS, July 12, 2007.

U.S. Navy, U.S. Marine Corps, U.S. Coast Guard. *A Cooperative Strategy for 21st Century Seapower.* Washington DC: October 2007.

U.S. Navy, U.S. Marine Corps, U.S. Coast Guard. *Naval Operations Concept 2010: Implementing the Maritime Strategy.* Washington, DC: 2010.

U.S. Government Accountability Office. *Additional Analysis and Oversight Required to Support the Navy's Future Surface Combatant Plans.* By Belva M. Martin. 2012 GAO-12-113. http://www.gao.gov/assets/590/587883.pdf.

U.S. Government Accountability Office. *Navy's Ability to Overcome Challenges Facing the Littoral Combat Ship Will Determine Eventual Capabilities,* by Belva M. Martin. 2010. GAO-10-523. http://www.gao.gov/new.items/d10523.pdf.

U.S. Government Accountability Office. *Challenges Associated with the Navy's Long-Range Shipbuilding Plan,* by Paul F. Francis. 2006. GAO-06-587T. http://www.gao.gov/assets/120/113284.pdf.

U.S. Government Accountability Office. *Actions Needed to Improve Operating Cost Estimates and Mitigating Risks in Implementing New Concepts,* by John H. Pendleton. 2010. GAO-10-257. http://www.gao.gov/new.items/d10257.pdf.

U.S. Government Accountability Office. *Improved Littoral War-Fighting Capabilities Needed,* by James F. Wiggins. 2001. GAO-01-493. http://www.gao.gov/assets/240/231703.pdf.

U.S. Government Accountability Office. *DOD Needs to Address Gaps in Homeland Defense and Civil Support Guidance,* by Brian J. Lepore. 2012. GAO-13-128. http://www.gao.gov/assets/650/649689.pdf.

U.S. Government Accountability Office. *DOD Can Enhance Efforts to Identify Capabilities to Support Civil Authorities during Disasters,* by Davi M. D'Agostino. GAO-10-386. 2010. http://www.gao.gov/new.items/d10386.pdf.

U.S. Government Accountability Office, *Portfolio Management Approach Needed to Improve Major Acquisitions Outcomes*, by John P. Hutton. 2012. GAO-12-918http://www.gao.gov/assets/650/648636.pdf.

U.S. Navy Africa Partnership Station. "About Africa Partnership Station." Accessed March 1, 2013. www.naveur-navaf.navy.mil\about%20us.html.

U.S. Navy. "The Carrier Strike Group." Accessed February 10, 2013. http://www.navy.mil/navydata/ships/carriers/powerhouse/cvbg.asp.

U.S. Navy. "The Amphibious Ready Group." May 29, 2009. Accessed February 10, 2013. http://www.navy.mil/navydata/nav_legacy.asp?id=148.

U.S. Navy. "Frigates – FFG." United States Navy Fact File. November 7, 2012. Accessed February 10, 2013. http://www.navy.mil/navydata/fact_display.asp?cid=4200&tid=1300&ct=4.

U.S. Navy. "Mine Countermeasure Ships – MCM." United States Navy Fact File. November 7, 2012. Accessed February 10, 2013. http://www.navy.mil/navydata/fact_display.asp?cid=4200&tid=1900&ct=4.

U.S. Navy. "Littoral Combat Ships – Mission Modules." United States Navy Fact File. October 25, 2012. Accessed February 10, 2013. http://www.navy.mil/navydata/fact_display.asp?cid=2100&tid=406&ct=2.

U.S. Navy. "Littoral Combat Ships – Surface Warfare (SUW) Mission Package." United States Navy Fact File. October 25, 2012. Accessed February 10, 2013. http://www.navy.mil/navydata/fact_display.asp?cid=2100&tid=437&ct=2.

U.S. Navy. "Littoral Combat Ships – Anti-Submarine Warfare (ASW) Mission Package." United States Navy Fact File. October 25, 2012. Accessed February 10, 2013. http://www.navy.mil/navydata/fact_display.asp?cid=2100&tid=412&ct=2.

U.S. Navy. "Littoral Combat Ships – Mine Countermeasures (MCM) Mission Package." United States Navy Fact File. October 25, 2012. Accessed February 10, 2013. http://www.navy.mil/navydata/fact_display.asp?cid=2100&tid=425&ct=2.

USNI News Editor. "Navy Defends Monday's LCS Contract Award." *USNI News*. March 3, 2013. Accessed March 5, 2013. http://news.usni.org/2013/03/05/navy-defends-mondays-lcs-contract-award.

USNI News Editor. "Navy Responds to Pentagon LCS Survivability Claims." *USNI News*. January 17, 2013. Accessed March 16, 2013. http://news.usni.org/2013/01/17/navy-responds-pentagon-lcs-survivability-claims.

"Valour class (Meko A-200 SAN) (FFGHM)." *IHS Jane's*. March 27, 2013.

"Visby class (FSGH)." *IHS Jane's.* November 16, 2011.

"Yemen Says Tanker Blast Was Terrorism." *BBC News.* October 16, 2002. Accessed March 1, 2013. http://news.bbc.co.uk/2/hi/middle_east/2334865.stm.

Walsh, Edward J. "Naval Systems-Navy Disputes LCS Criticisms." *Proceedings Magazine*, June 2012. Accessed February 21, 2013. http://www.usni.org/magazines/proceedings/2012-06/naval-systems-navy-disputes-lcs-criticisms.

Watts, Robert B. "The New Normalcy: Sea Power and Contingency Operations in the Twenty-First Century." *Naval War College Review 65, no. 3* (Summer 2012): 47-64.

Vego, Milan. "No Need for High Speed." *Proceedings Magazine*, September 2009. Accessed February 21, 2013. http://www.usni.org/magazines/proceedings/2009-09/no-need-high-speed.

INITIAL DISTRIBUTION LIST

1. Defense Technical Information Center
    Ft. Belvoir, Virginia

2. Dudley Knox Library
    Naval Postgraduate School
    Monterey, California

www.ingramcontent.com/pod-product-compliance
Lightning Source LLC
Chambersburg PA
CBHW050620110426
42813CB00010B/2620